THE
WELL-CENTERED
HOME

THE
WELL-CENTERED
HOME

SIMPLE STEPS *to* INCREASE MINDFULNESS,
SELF-AWARENESS, *and* HAPPINESS
WHERE YOU LIVE

WILLIAM HIRSCH AIA

Author of Amazon #1 Bestseller, *Designing Your Perfect House*

Printed in the United States of America

First Printing, 2020

ISBN: 978-0-9884149-2-1 (paperback)
ISBN 978-0-9884149-3-8 (ebook)

Library of Congress Cataloguing Number: 2020909586

Published by:
William J. Hirsch Jr.,
Callawassie Island, South Carolina

Cover and Interior Book Design by: Redwood Publishing, LLC

Disclaimer: Although the author and publisher have made every effort to ensure that the information in this book was correct at press time, the author and publisher do not assume and hereby disclaim any liability to any party for any loss, damage, or disruption caused by errors or omissions, whether such errors or omissions result from negligence, accident, or any other cause.

10 9 8 7 6 5 4 3 2 1

Contents

Dedication

This book is dedicated to all my clients who gave me the opportunity to explore architectural design and to learn that a well-centered home is a safe haven for the spirit, a catalyst to rejuvenate the psyche, and much more than just a structure to keep out the weather.

Acknowledgements

No one writes and publishes a book completely on their own. This book is no exception. The hard work of several creative people came together to make it possible. In particular, I would like to thank Elizabeth Trach, whose collaboration made this book what it is. Michael Levin provided much need guidance and encouragement. Marnie Gowan provided the icon graphics. Sara Stratton is responsible for the cover and interior layout of the book. And then there is my family, especially my wife, Maureen, who helped keep things on track. I appreciate everyone's efforts.

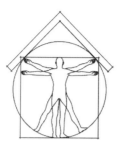

Chapter 1

WHY YOU'LL BE HAPPIER AND HEALTHIER IN A WELL-CENTERED HOME

Your home has an enormous impact on your emotional well-being. It's the place where you spend most of your time, but have you given much thought to how your spirit interacts with the physical structure and arrangement of your home? If you haven't, you're not alone. Most people who grow up in Western culture tend to think of a house or apartment as simply a building that provides protection from the elements. It is a shell to be filled with possessions and decorated in a certain style. There's nothing wrong with that, but a well-centered home is so much more.

That's because your home has the power to channel or repel the energy that nourishes you. It can energize and recharge you. It can increase your mindfulness and help you feel at peace. When you learn to recognize and focus the flow of energy, you can design your home to bring you psychological benefits that help you thrive just by living in your space. These benefits are something you can feel when you enter into a well-centered home, but—in Western culture, at least—we often lack the language to describe what we're experiencing. And when we don't have words, the ideas tend to linger below the surface, curled up in our subconscious.

I find it helps to think of the energy in your home like another familiar but also invisible kind of energy: radio waves. Radio waves have always been there, but it's only been since the late 1800s that they've been understood enough to use in communication. As with gravity, electricity, microwaves, and magnetism, scientists eventually learned to harness the power of forces we can't see, but that act on us all the time. There is still much be learned about other forms of energy that pulse through our world and the universe.

The energy in your home is a bit like the once-mysterious energy of radio waves. It's there, but you have to learn to control it. And without a proper receiver such as a radio or cellphone, you cannot detect this energy or tune in to the correct frequency. It remains unintelligible static. Now that we know how to control and receive radio waves, inventions like radios, cellphones, and Wi-Fi have all become an indispensable part of our lives.

A well-centered home "tunes in" to the universal energy that flows through us and through the world around us, focusing it in a way that provides benefits to its inhabitants. Western cultures don't readily recognize this, but Eastern cultures have addressed energy in building design for a long time. Feng shui is a great example of a centuries-old home planning philosophy that seeks to explain these forces and how they work in your home. The thing that architects call the "built environment"—that is, the buildings and objects we interact with—has a dramatic impact on us that goes beyond physical comfort. Westerners aren't consciously aware of it, but that doesn't mean it doesn't happen.

So think of this book as your manual to understanding and harnessing the energy in your home to make you feel perfectly at ease and well-centered when you arrive. You'll learn to tune in to the energy in your home, just as a radio receiver lets you tune in to your favorite station. As you begin to understand the energy, you'll be able to make adjustments that allow your home to be the most comfortable, restorative, energizing, and calming place to live your best life.

THE CONCEPT OF CENTERING

In meditation, the practice of centering is about being present in time and space. It is mindfulness of the moment, rather than worrying about the future or dwelling on the past. When you're centered, you feel recharged emotionally and spiritually.

To understand what centering feels like, consider a soap bubble. The soap bubble is perfectly spherical because the pressures within the bubble are exactly equal throughout. The air pressure pushing out is the same as the pressure pushing in, and all is in balance. If an outside force distorts the bubble into an irregular shape, the bubble will not remain in that new shape for long. It always settles back into a perfect sphere. That is its natural state.

The universe is like that soap bubble. Everything in nature resolves to a point of balance. But nothing is static. The sun comes up and the sun goes down. Tides rise and fall. Seasons come and go and come again. Nature is always moving in cycles, and fluctuations occur, but eventually balance is achieved. The universe and the world we live in exist in a state of dynamic equilibrium.

Our consciousness is also just like the soap bubble. Our daily lives are full of external forces—traffic jams, angry bosses, crying babies—that distort our bubble, but the bubble always wants to return to its spherical shape. When our personal bubble is nested concentrically inside the universe's bubble, we are balanced and in harmony. Nothing pushes against us, and we feel comfortable, peaceful, and at rest.

The well-centered home helps restore and protect your personal bubble of well-being. Humans are directly influenced and shaped by our environment. The built environment—in this case, our home—can either distort our personal sphere or it can help us resolve into the perfect shape we desire.

Is Home-Centering the Same as Feng Shui?

Home-centering is not feng shui, though the two practices overlap to some degree. Both practices share the common goal of creating a harmonious home environment that benefits and energizes those who dwell within. Where the two disciplines differ is in the ease of application, the rigidity of the principles, and the freedom to customize the home to match the taste of its occupants.

Feng shui requires strict adherence to prescribed principles, including arranging furniture according to the *bagua*, a specialized map that divides the home into nine segments. These ancient guidelines apply to all homes and are designed to channel universal energy

continued on the next page...

Is Home-Centering the Same as Feng Shui?

...continued

into them in ways that bring health and fortune to their residents. The expectation is that you bring your home into compliance with the rules of feng shui. Because it's such a complex practice, countless books have been written on the subject, and many feng shui devotees retain an expert to guide them in the process of aligning their home's energy.

Home-centering, on the other hand, considers the home's occupants first—their unique needs, desires, and personalities—and suggests modifications to improve the power of the home to bring happiness and mindfulness to its occupants. The energy of a well-centered home synchronizes with the spiritual energy of its occupants to create a place of harmony and peace. The well-centered home is tailored to the needs of the people living there and therefore provides an engaging, gratifying experience for all who enter.

WHAT IS THE WELL-CENTERED HOME?

The well-centered home is one that has been adjusted and fine-tuned so that it becomes a place that helps you become centered. It is one in which rough spots and negative influences have been removed and the flow of energy has been improved so that the home fulfills its restorative purpose. The well-centered home performs the same task as meditation to ground and center you, but it does so in the background. You receive the benefits simply by living there.

You will learn in this book that the well-centered home:

- Provides a centering place in which you are free to live in the moment

- Eliminates friction in the form of distraction and daily annoyances

- Recharges you emotionally as your subconscious self creates a healthy relationship with your home

- Flows smoothly and is free of obstructions that hinder body and spirit

- Recognizes, reinforces, and resonates with life's natural rhythms to promote balance

- Is dynamic and changing, not static or rigid

- Is both anchored to the earth and open to the sky

- Is designed to fit *your* personality and lifestyle, not a prescribed idea of style

In a well-centered home, everything feels *right*. Many things contribute to this, including appropriate colors, a sense of scale, and a sense of fluid movement. In almost all the houses I've designed, I've looked for opportunities to present a view that captures your attention as you move about the space. For example, you may round a corner on the way to the bedroom and be presented with a work of art, or perhaps a Zen window that frames a lovely view. When properly arranged, this moment triggers your inner consciousness to go directly to that object, and you become less aware of your physical body as you walk along your path. That shedding of the consciousness is similar to what meditation does, and you are freer to enjoy living.

The way we design and arrange our homes really does have the power to do this. We often think only in terms of our five senses—sight, hearing, touch, taste, and smell—but humans are sensitive to many other influences. For example, we have a sense of appropriate scale that dictates our comfort in certain places. Standing alone on the floor of an empty basketball arena creates a distinctly uncomfortable feeling for most of us because the scale of the space is far too cavernous for one person. On the other hand, a restaurant booth is a sought-after seat because it perfectly fits a group of four and provides a bit of coziness in an otherwise open restaurant.

We may lack language for some of the feelings that architecture inspires in us, but scientists are beginning to measure these effects. For example, studies have shown that patients in hospital rooms with views of nature heal faster and have fewer complications than those who had a view of a brick wall. When no natural view is possible, even having access to artwork that depicts nature helps to reduce anxiety and lower pain responses.[1] Architecture has the power to influence how we feel, so why not harness that power in our homes?

THE BENEFITS OF A WELL-CENTERED HOME

The primary purpose of creating a well-centered home is to improve your emotional well-being. The well-centered home nudges you in the direction of happiness and provides a space where you can be emotionally and mentally present.

In the medical world, doctors observe the Hippocratic oath: First, do no harm. Taking care of your emotional well-being through architecture is similar in that the first step is to remove the harmful elements of an unbalanced home. In the case of your home, harmful elements are things that create disturbances to your peace of mind. Some are obvious, like replacing burned-out light bulbs in a dim hallway. The lack of light you experience on your path through this area draws your attention, either consciously or subconsciously, away from your purpose and causes you to feel irritated and unhappy. Solving this problem eliminates

---

[1] Franklin, Deborah. "How Hospital Gardens Help Patients Heal," *Scientific American*, March 1, 2012, https://www.scientificamerican.com/article/nature-that-nurtures/

the aggravation and allows you to continue living your life, smoothing the path before you and creating that feeling of balance.

Of course, not all disturbances are as easy to recognize— if they were, we'd all be living in well-centered homes (with fully operational light bulbs) already! But consider the example of the light bulbs. Replacing the bulbs will remove a disturbance, but there's also an opportunity to *improve* the lighting so it has a positive impact on you. Will you choose bulbs that emit harsh, agitating light, or will you choose bulbs with a warmer color temperature that softens the space and adds a welcoming glow to that hallway? You may not be consciously aware of it, but most people are quite sensitive to the color temperature of their bulbs, and making this simple change can help you relax at home—instead of feeling like you're trapped in an office with greenish-blue fluorescent lighting.

And don't worry if you're not familiar with color temperature and light bulb types—I'll talk more about how to work with lighting to channel your home's energy in Chapter 10.

As the simple example of the light bulb shows, the well-centered home offers practical benefits, as well as some that are less readily definable. Removing disturbances and creating balance often involves making your home function better. From fixing a leaky faucet to remove the annoying sound of the drip to organizing your mudroom to make mornings more seamless, the well-centered home supports you in your daily activities in endless practical ways.

Finally, there are aesthetic benefits to the well-centered home. These are closely related to the emotional benefits, as beauty makes people feel good. But in the well-centered home, beauty arises from harmony and balance. No particular style or look dictates the layout of the home—instead, the home is designed to serve the emotional and practical needs of the people living in it.

Too often, architects are trained to design objects. They're obsessed with materials and geometric forms, which leads to making buildings or homes that are just avant garde sculptures. They're incredible to look at, but they're completely detached from the needs of the people who inhabit them. Open up any magazine devoted to modern home design, and you'll see what I mean. It's beautiful, but often unlivable.

In my view, architecture should be about understanding the type and quality of space we want to live in and how we want to feel inside of it. The purpose of the architect is to define the edges of that space and give it a tangible shape and character—not just to build a beautiful shell. Architecture is much more than merely a giant sculpture. The well-centered home is a place that harnesses the energy around you to suit your needs. In some places, it will delight and energize you; in others, it will calm and restore you. But always, *you* are at the center of the well-centered home.

Meet the Architect

Whenever I meet someone looking to work with an architect, I always recommend that they get to know them first—it's the only way to develop a real partnership. And since, in picking up this book, you're working with me, I'd like to introduce myself.

In college as an undergraduate, I majored in psychology because I have always been interested in how people see the world, and especially what makes them feel happy and fulfilled. I later graduated from the University of Virginia with a master's degree in architecture. While I was there I had the pleasure of working with a wonderful professor who took the approach that architecture is for people—period. His ideas spoke to me, and from that class onward I have always worked to understand the people who would be living in the space I designed. We work together to define what home means to them. My greatest thrill is when clients tell me their new house feels like *their* home.

In my nearly 50-year career, I've designed just about everything, including office, commercial, religious, recreational, and industrial buildings. But my true passion is designing homes for individuals and families. In this work I get to put people first, which to my mind is exactly as it should be.

ANYONE CAN ACHIEVE A WELL-CENTERED HOME

Though I have spent a career thinking about how architects can create a well-centered home, the ideas in this book don't require an expert to carry out. *Everyone* can work to make their home a restorative place that provides the right energy for living well. The well-centered home doesn't require an architect or a big budget to achieve. It doesn't even require a permanent address or a traditional house—renters, condo owners, and college students can all achieve balance and harmony in their homes.

For example, let's consider a studio apartment. As a renter, the terms of your lease may restrict what you're allowed to do in your space. You may not be able to paint the walls to add a soothing color, but you *can* adjust the furnishings and add accessories to build a harmonious palette that way. Furniture is a very important way for renters to take control of the energy in their homes: its arrangement, its lines and its colors can all work together to transform and center a room.

Likewise, city dwellers living on the fifth floor (or higher!) might wonder how they can get in touch with nature in their high-rise. What do you do when every view is a cityscape, with no trees in sight? Hospital studies have shown us that artwork and images of nature can bring almost as much peace and healing to a room as nature itself, so don't worry: there's plenty you can do to create your oasis, and we'll address ways to get earth-grounded in Chapter 3.

The point is that you don't have to spend an enormous amount of money or effort to center your home. As you learn to identify and work with the energy in your living space, you'll be able to make changes that affect you on a subconscious level and make you feel more comfortable every day.

Of course, if you're looking to renovate or add on to your home, you can also do that in a way that supports the well-centered home. From adding windows that connect you to the open sky to designing a room to serve as a cozy, restful getaway from the noise of the day, there are so many ways to adjust the architecture of your home to serve your needs.

It is my hope, then, that this book serves as inspiration for you as you begin your journey. The more you learn about the energy in your home, the more you will ultimately learn about yourself, the universe, and your place within it.

HOW TO USE THIS BOOK

Because the well-centered home is all about you, we'll begin with a quiz designed to help you consider your needs and preferences for living. This is the jumping-off point for looking around your current dwelling to decide what works for you—and what needs to be brought into balance.

In each chapter, we'll look at an architectural concept to see how it affects your well-being in your home. I'll explain some important concepts from Eastern philosophies, including feng shui, Balinese ideology, and Vastu to illustrate how our homes influence our thoughts and emotions. I'll also introduce some of my own terms and ideas that I've developed in my practice as an architect to help you adjust and center your home.

This isn't all about theory. Each chapter will be filled with practical, doable tips and advice to show you how to improve your home's energy. There's something in here for everyone, whether you have a $0 budget or mad money to play with, and tips are coded by cost ($, $$, or $$$). When you see a tip you like, feel free to mark it with a sticky note, or dog-ear the page so you can come back to it when you're ready to put what you've learned into practice.

Remember, your home's size, location, and style can neither help nor hinder you when it comes to centering. It honestly doesn't matter. Instead, we'll be focused on how to remove irritations and optimize your connection to nature and your sense of well-being. Once you know how to work with the energy that's all around you, the well-centered home is within your reach.

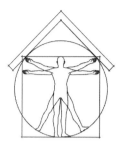

Chapter 2

WHAT TYPE OF HOMEBODY ARE YOU? A 20-QUESTION QUIZ

A well-centered home must be personalized for each individual. Some people are attracted to groups, and others prefer a more solitary existence. The goal of a well-centered home is to harness its energy to support your personality—but first, you need to understand your needs and preferences.

To help you look inward and evaluate your tendencies, I've developed a twenty-question personality quiz. Considering each of the questions carefully will reveal aspects of your personality that you should honor as you design your well-centered home.

It's important to remember that there are no right or wrong answers to these questions. The goal isn't to pigeonhole you into a certain style—indeed, no one is 100 percent one homebody type, but rather a uniquely proportioned mix of each. You may find that your answers change over time, given short-term changes in your mood and long-term changes in your personal style. The purpose of this quiz is to help you recognize your general tendencies so you can focus on ways to center your home that will best resonate with your personality.

HOW TO TAKE THIS QUIZ

If you don't want to write in the book, make a quick answer sheet on scrap paper. Number it 1–20 and write the letter of the answer that best resonates with you for each.

It's best to choose one answer for each question, but if you're occasionally torn between two, it's okay to choose both. Remember, the point isn't to dismiss any of your tastes. It's to identify them so you can use them to your advantage as you work to center your home.

The Homebody Type Quiz

1. On weekends or holidays, I most look forward to:

    ____a) Lively group activities like team sports or parties.

    ____b) Going on a bike ride or outing alone or with my immediate family.

    ____c) Visiting a friend or family member who needs my help.

    ____d) Tidying up my home and checking things off my to-do list.

2. When viewing artwork, I find myself:

    ____a) Looking at its price tag and thinking how that money could be put to better use.

    ____b) Focusing on the colors, shapes, and textures to decide if I like it.

    ____c) Analyzing its composition and wondering about the artist's intention.

    ____d) Considering how the object was made and the technical skill required.

3. When a friend or relative tells me about a problem in their life, my first instinct is to:

    ____a) Change the subject to something less depressing.

    ____b) Understand the problem, offer suggestions, and find solutions.

___c) Listen patiently and suggest professionals who can best help.

___d) Offer comfort, encouragement, and emotional support.

4. If you open up my notebook, you'll see:

___a) Carefully aligned lists, bullet points, and outlines.

___b) Complete sentences and comments about how items may affect others.

___c) Lots of arrows, asterisks, and doodles. I jot things down when the mood strikes.

___d) A balance of facts and my own thoughts about them.

5. When I have an idea to improve something at work or home, I:

___a) Focus on helping people and work backward from that desired outcome as I plan.

___b) Work out all the details on my own before mentioning it to anyone.

___c) Play devil's advocate and try to pick my idea apart, to see if it holds up.

___d) Share my thoughts with others to gauge their reactions and get help as I continue to develop my idea.

6. When it comes to entertainment, I tend to choose:

_____a) Nonfiction books, documentaries, and historical movies.

_____b) Live performances, plays, and music festivals.

_____c) Books and movies in which the protagonist strives to achieve a higher purpose.

_____d) Movies, books, and TV shows with a heartwarming theme and a happy ending.

7. When asked for my opinion, I tend to:

_____a) Answer in a humorous or clever way.

_____b) Consider the consequences of my answer but still answer honestly.

_____c) Answer candidly, regardless of whether others disagree or not. No apologies.

_____d) Phrase my answer tactfully so that I don't create an argument, even if I disagree with someone.

8. I am happiest when my activities are:

_____a) Helpful to others and make people happy.

_____b) Spontaneous and unplanned. Impromptu get-togethers energize me.

_____c) Meaningful and improve life for me and for others.

_____d) Scheduled in advance. Impromptu events are disruptive to me.

9. I do my best, most effective work when:

___a) My work is meaningful and I have time to think things through.

___b) I know my work will have a positive impact.

___c) My schedule is full and my work is in public or with a team.

___d) I can complete my tasks in private, where I can concentrate.

10. I wake up in the morning looking forward to a day:

___a) Without surprises, so I can accomplish the goals I've set.

___b) That offers new opportunities to expand my horizons.

___c) That brings peace and calm to my loved ones and myself.

___d) Packed with interesting new challenges to energize me.

11. If asked to describe myself, I would say that I tend to be:

___a) Introspective. I like to understand the reasons why things happen and what they mean.

___b) Encouraging. I like to help people get along with each other and show my appreciation of them.

____c) Tenacious. I stand by my beliefs and get things done.

____d) Optimistic. I try to look at the bright side of life.

12. Work goes best when:

____a) Rules and schedules are followed and everyone stays on task.

____b) There is a clear leader who takes charge and encourages the group.

____c) There is room for innovation and a willingness to experiment.

____d) There are good team dynamics and everyone contributes.

13. When talking to friends and colleagues, I often:

____a) Keep my opinions to myself to avoid saying things others might disagree with.

____b) Express my ideas and invite others to share theirs, even if we disagree.

____c) Tend to dominate the conversation. I don't mean to, but I have strong opinions.

____d) Question what others say and ask them for evidence.

14. When I have a quiet moment, I tend to think about:

____a) My own life and activities. I take a realistic view of things and tend to live in the present.

____b) My community and the world at large. I look forward to the future and like to speculate about it.

____c) The big problems in the world and how they might be solved.

____d) the meaning of life and my special purpose.

15. If asked to be a referee or judge in a contest, I would:

____a) Accept the job and apply the rules as written to the best of my understanding.

____b) Decline the job because I would have trouble assessing penalties and feel bad for the losing side.

____c) Accept the job but apply the rules in a way that does not interfere with the flow of the game or the players' enjoyment.

____d) Accept the job and express my personality in the process.

16. When I am planning a family vacation, I create:

____a) A schedule that includes activities for everyone, as well as time to relax.

___b) A plan that takes us to interesting natural and historic sites.

___c) A detailed itinerary with pre-purchased tickets, reservations, and a schedule that maximizes our time.

___d) A rough schedule that leaves room for improvisation and leisure time. I like serendipitous discoveries.

17. When I have purchased something that requires assembly, I usually:

___a) Find myself considering how it was made and how it was designed to fit together.

___b) Glance at the parts and skim the instructions. I'll only refer back to them if I get stuck.

___c) Get someone to help me, then go bake cookies for them as a thank you.

___d) Lay out all the parts to make sure everything is there, read the instructions, and then assemble step-by-step as directed.

18. As a general rule, I value:

___a) Facts and proven experience. I like to see the world as it is.

___b) Theories and hope for the future. I like to envision what might be.

____c) Optimism and self-expression. I like to be myself.

____d) Caring and generosity. It's better to help others than to help yourself.

19. I prefer a job or career that lets me:

____a) Get out of the office and engage with people.

____b) Build upon facts to create positive outcomes.

____c) Comfort and guide people to feeling happy and secure.

____d) Have a purpose beyond simply punching the time clock.

20. If I decided to make a pancake breakfast, I would:

____a) Make sure the griddle is the perfect temperature and use a measured scoop, so pancakes come out a uniform size.

____b) Pour the batter onto the griddle in clever ways to create snowmen and animals to entertain the kids.

____c) Use organic, unprocessed, natural ingredients and toppings.

____d) Work quickly and not worry about appearances, so I can keep everyone's plate full.

HOW TO TALLY YOUR RESULTS

Circle the letter (or possibly letters) you chose for each question. Then add the number of circles you have in each column (Astaire, Galileo, Nightingale and Plato) and write the total at the bottom. Again, if you prefer not to write in the book, you can make a tally sheet on a piece of scrap paper.

Question	Astaire	Galileo	Nightingale	Plato
1	a	d	c	b
2	b	d	a	c
3	a	c	d	b
4	c	a	b	d
5	d	b	a	c
6	b	a	d	c
7	a	c	d	b
8	b	d	a	c
9	c	d	b	a
10	d	a	c	b
11	d	c	b	a
12	b	a	d	c
13	c	d	a	b
14	a	b	c	d
15	d	a	b	c
16	d	c	a	b
17	b	d	c	a
18	c	a	d	b
19	a	b	c	d
20	b	a	d	c
Total				

Now look at your scores. The column with the highest point total is your dominant homebody type. The second-highest score is your homebody tendency. For example, you may be a dominant Plato with Nightingale tendencies.

Remember, most people are a mix of all four homebody types, and you're likely to recognize a bit of each type in yourself. But understanding your dominant types will help you focus your energy in ways that make you feel at home as you work to center your living space.

THE HOMEBODY PERSONALITY TYPES

 ### Astaire: The Entertainer

> *"If it doesn't look easy, it's that we haven't tried hard enough yet."*

Fred Astaire was an iconic American dancer, singer, and actor in the golden age of Hollywood movie musicals. A highly respected professional, he was a perfectionist when it came to his craft and delighted in entertaining his audience.

Like its namesake, the Astaire homebody type favors elegance and refinement, and thrives on entertaining others in their home.

Hallmarks of the Astaire homebody type:

- Loves to play host and entertain guests

- Dislikes being alone; is energized by large groups

- Enjoys high-energy interactions but dislikes chaos

- Is equally comfortable at home or in larger community spaces

- Prefers carefully designed indoor spaces to the outdoors

- Favors bright lights and colors

- Appreciates rhythms and patterns in visuals and in music

- Requires shapes and lines to flow together harmoniously

- Prefers furnishings that create a focal point or make a statement

- Enjoys accessories that give life to furnishings and create conversation

- Is energized by glass and bright or brushed metals

- Prefers a simple but rich color palette: deep blues or plum, subtle yellows, and white with orange or red accents

- Is sensitive to "sour notes" in design and decor

Quick Tip

Astaire homebody types love to entertain, so make sure your rooms are set up to encourage conversation. Try rearranging living room seating in a U shape or with two sofas facing each other instead of the TV. In the dining room, a bright centerpiece on the table can help focus diners' attention on the meal instead of their phones.

Galileo: The Scientist

"To understand the universe, you must first understand the language in which it's written, the language of mathematics."

Galileo Galilei was an Italian astronomer, physicist, and engineer during the Renaissance. He believed that science held the answers to questions about the universe, and he caused a sea change in belief when he proved that the earth orbited the sun, instead of the other way around.

The Galileo homebody type prefers logic and order in all things. This type is passionate about understanding how things work and craves efficiency at home.

Hallmarks of the Galileo homebody type:

- Is comfortable alone or in groups, as long as interactions are planned

- Works best in quiet and solitude

- Resists change unless there's a strong reason behind it

- Is comfortable in a controlled, orderly environment

- Appreciates indoor-outdoor spaces with spots for quiet thinking

- Requires appropriate task lighting

- Favors geometric shapes and symmetry

- Requires shapes and lines of decor to flow together harmoniously

- Prefers durable, functional furnishings that provide a sense of grounding

- Enjoys decor that is also useful, such as clocks or maps

- Feels comforted by muted colors and natural materials

- Is energized by a simplified, more monochromatic color palette

- Is sensitive to clutter and extraneous items that don't serve a purpose

Quick Tip

Galileo homebody types need a place to sit and work out their big ideas about the world and how it works. Try placing a reading chair and ottoman in the corner of quiet room. Place it at a 45-degree angle so the walls form protective "blinders" in your peripheral vision that allow you to focus on the book or other project in front of you.

Nightingale: The Nurturer

> *"The object and color in the materials around us actually have a physical effect on us, on how we feel."*

Florence Nightingale left behind a life of Victorian privilege to devote herself to nursing. Sent to care for the wounded during the Crimean War, she sprang into action to heal the wounded and began a lifelong career. Much of her work was dedicated to improving conditions of the hospitals to transform them into sanitary, healing spaces.

The Nightingale homebody type is a nurturer who enjoys caring for the physical and emotional needs of friends and family. They put people first and thrive in spaces that, above all, provide comfort.

Hallmarks of the Nightingale homebody type:

- Prefers socializing in intimate groups

- Avoids the spotlight and prefers teamwork

- Prefers the home to be an unchanging, safe harbor

- Values cleanliness but can tolerate higher doses of chaos than most

- Appreciates healthful fresh air and sunshine

- Enjoys the warmth of the sun and soft mood lighting

- Prefers curved forms and flowing lines

- Values materials and surfaces that are easy to keep clean

- Prefers soft, comfortable furniture and plush accessories

- Enjoys decor that has sentimental value or personal meaning

- Enjoys earth tones and soft yellows, greens, and teal shades

- May wish to avoid red, except in soft tones or small accents

- Feels oppressed by dim lighting, dirt, and stuffy, stale rooms

 Quick Tip

Nightingale homebody types live to make others feel comfortable and well cared for. You can instantly make any seating area more welcoming by adding decorative pillows in soft fabrics like microfiber or chenille. When the weather turns cool, have several blankets or throws available for guests to cuddle up into.

Plato: The Philosopher

"Man is the measure of all things."

One of the most famous ancient Greek philosophers, Plato pondered the relationship between perception and reality. He did not accept things at face value, but rather sought to understand the meaning of life by digging beyond forms to understand abstract truths. He was also a beloved teacher who challenged his students to think for themselves.

The Plato homebody type is a deep thinker who seeks to understand the world. While a Galileo type works to understand *how* things work, the Plato type prefers to ask *why*. They enjoy conversation and want their home to be an anchoring point from which to explore their ideas.

Hallmarks of the Plato homebody type:

- Has a limited tolerance for guests, but enjoys thoughtful discussion

- Values quiet time for contemplation

- Is open to change and innovation

- Dislikes chaos and prefers clean vistas with a singular focal point

- Prefers home to be a secure vantage point from which to view nature

- Prefers natural light and a connection to daily and seasonal sun cycles

- Appreciates irregular forms and shapes that provoke thought

- Favors materials that indicate permanence, such as stone, iron, and blocks of wood

- Appreciates textures and objects with interesting features

- Prefers furnishings with a history

- Enjoys decor that features craftsmanship and skill

- Responds to colors that unite earth and sky: a balance of brown, blue, and green

- Is bothered by distracting sounds and visual "busyness"

Quick Tip

Plato homebody types like to feel connected to history and contemplate their place in time and space. A stack of classic books, a framed black-and-white photo of an ancestor, or an antique reading lamp are good additions to a desk or den where the Plato will escape for a meditative moment.

TRANSLATING SELF-KNOWLEDGE INTO ACTION

Now that you have a deeper understanding of your personality and how it informs your preferences, it's time to use what you've learned. As you continue reading, you'll learn more about how to craft your space to make you feel safe, supported, and balanced. You'll also find specific tips for ways to harness your home's energy based on your personality. Be sure to look for your personality icon throughout the book to find advice tailored specifically to you.

Are you ready to embrace your well-centered home? Let's begin.

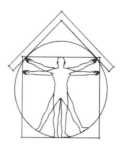

Chapter 3

YOUR HOME IN THE UNIVERSE: ANCHORING, GROUNDING, AND CONNECTING WITH THE SUN AND THE MOON

A
s you begin the process of centering your home, it's important to understand how your home functions as your foundational place in the universe. It is the central point around which your world revolves. It is your point of reference, retreat, and restoration.

On one level, your home is physical, of course. It's the brick-and-mortar shelter that protects you from the elements. But centering your home requires that you see your home as a spiritual place as well.

The concept of home is expressed differently in various parts of the world, but some consistencies persist. In many cultures, deities are believed to inhabit the place above us, while malevolent beings live in the place below. We humans live in the "in between." In the early days of Western cultures, Greek gods and goddesses looked down on humans from their vantage point on Mount Olympus, while the dead crossed the River Styx into Hades below. Christian ideas of angels in heaven and devils and demons in hell also fit into this model. Humans, in the meantime, live in between these two realms. All life on earth is situated at the midpoint between the sacred above and the profane below.

It's not only Western civilizations that adopted this concept. In Bali and other mountainous island cultures, the separation of *above* and *below* is also quite clear, perhaps because the world of an island society is so clearly condensed in space. Life-giving fresh water comes from the cloud-wrapped mountains above in the form of rain, waterfalls, and rivers flowing from the mountaintop. As the pure water passes through human households and villages, it nourishes. It also becomes dirtied through use, and eventually carries refuse downhill and out to sea—the depths of which were dark and unknown. Seen this way, living in-between isn't just an allegory: It's a foundational fact of human existence.

So where does that leave you, the reader in search of a well-centered home? You too live in the in-between place. We all do. Your home is your sanctuary and the link between *above* and *below*. Powerful universal energy passes through this realm, and our homes must channel that energy and deliver it to us in a way that helps us recharge and restore our psyches. We need to feel safe from the profane, connected to the sacred, and securely anchored in our place in between. When our homes become centered, we become centered.

Your home is the balance point between two equally important forces in the universe: the physical and the spiritual. We're already quite accustomed to thinking of our homes in a physical way: a collection of bricks and shingles that protect our bodies. But a well-centered home also provides for our spiritual needs by providing a nourishing space to rest, recover, and rejuvenate.

To begin to work effectively with both the physical and spiritual nature of your home, you'll need to understand four important concepts: anchoring, earth-grounding, solar orienting, and lunar orienting.

Bali in Harmony with the Universe

On the Indonesian island of Bali, architecture is rooted in a worldview that presents the universe as an integrated whole—a place in which each part is connected to and participates in the existence of every other

continued on the next page...

Bali in Harmony with the Universe

...continued

part. A Balinese house is seen as a smaller representation of the island and the universe as a whole, so the home is meant to recreate the harmony between humans and the rest of the universe.

The Balinese people view the universe as being divided into three domains: *buhr,* the underworld and domain of evil spirits; *bhuwah,* the earth and domain of humans; and *swah,* the heavens above and domain of the gods and deified ancestors. Balinese architecture mimics this arrangement by placing the sacred parts of the home on the uphill side of the house, the human parts in the center, and the unclean parts of the house on the downhill side. This allows the energy that flows down the mountain from the gods to be pure when it reaches the home, become polluted as it passes through the domain of the humans, and be further dirtied as it flows on to the sea, where the malevolent spirits reside.

Rooms and spaces in the home are arranged relative to this flow, relative to points of the compass, and measured relative to the size of parts of the owner's body, such as forearms and feet. This maintains a harmonious relationship with the universe to bring good fortune and a good life.

ANCHORING

Anchoring your home means understanding, on a deep, personal level, where your home is located in the universe. We've already discussed how your home is in an in-between space between the physical and the spiritual, but truly anchoring your home requires knowing its position on earth and conceptualizing its place in the universe.

Of course, you already know your address, but how *aware* of your home's position are you? Could you accurately point north right now? Do you know where the sun comes up in the morning and where it sets in the evening?

Most people struggle with these basics, especially as we become more dependent on GPS to find our way around. But developing a strong sense of where you're located provides a subliminal sense of security that enhances your feeling of being at home in your space. We have all experienced the uncomfortable feeling of being lost. It's disorienting and causes anxiety. When you do find a landmark and restore your grasp of your location, there's an immediate flood of relief and calm.

Let your home be that landmark in your life.

One important way to do this is to make your home stand out. Imagine driving through a neighborhood in which all the houses are similar. It's hard to find your way. The same is true for an apartment in a building where every door looks just like the others. You'll make your home a much more solid place by personalizing your entryway—and the rest of your home—so it speaks to you.

Anchoring begins with awareness. Right now, use a compass (there are free apps for that) to determine your home's orientation on the planet. Learn to point north, south, east, and west. Then open a map or navigation app and zoom out to see where your house is in relation to work, school, family, friends, and any other center of the community that's important to you. Physically point in their direction as if you could see them through the walls, naming them as you go. It may feel silly at first, but this exercise will help you discover and internalize your place in your town—a crucial first step in centering your home. Then zoom out to see where your town is relative to your county, state, or region. Next, remind yourself where you are situated in your country, then your continent, and finally on the planet.

EARTH-GROUNDING

While anchoring is about understanding your position in the universe, **earth-grounding** requires you to connect your home with nature. This concept is closely related to anchoring in that both provide a sense of security and stability in your home that allow you to feel emotionally calm and collected when you are there.

Connecting to nature came naturally to our ancient ancestors, who were necessarily living closer to the elements. They slept first in caves and later in simple homes built of felled logs or with earthen or thatched roofs, and they felt the heat and the cold far more than we do today. Today we live in man-made environments that are insulated and isolated from nature. Most of our surroundings—from the computer screens we stare at to the chair we sit in—come from a factory. While we may be more physically comfortable, living at a remove from the natural world means missing out on its calming, healing presence. Earth-grounding provides for your home the same sense of connection and stability that the practice of grounding does in meditation practice.

The best way to make your home more earth-grounded is to add or improve views of nature. As an exercise, take stock of all your home's natural views by temporarily uncovering all of your windows. Live with the views for several days and see how they make you feel. Are there views that consistently make you pause as you move from room to room? Are you able to enjoy the motion of fluttering leaves or flitting birds? Or do your views leave something to be desired? These connections are critically important, even if they only occur briefly as you move from room to room. Several quick glances outdoors as you move through your home can be just as beneficial as a long, lingering gaze.

For many people, earth-grounding is as simple as reconsidering the window treatments to frame the view of the back yard, but you can also substitute artwork that depicts nature if you don't have a suitable view. Successful earth-grounding addresses all your senses, so consider adding the sounds of flowing water or plants with a scent you enjoy. It's also possible to address earth-grounding in more subtle ways by choosing furnishings and decor made of natural materials like wood and rattan instead of man-made glass and metal.

 Quick Tip

An easy way to address anchoring and earth-grounding at the same time is with a wreath on your front door. It makes your home easily recognizable and instantly adds a touch of nature to your threshold. Is it any wonder that wreaths have been essential decor for over 500 years?[2]

From Bauhaus to the Well-Centered Home

My academic education, like that of many architects, revolved around the culture of the Bauhaus, the quintessential school of

continued on the next page...

---

[2] Moon, Kat. "Christmas Wreaths Are a Classic Holiday Decoration With a Surprisingly Deep History." *Time.* 21 Dec. 2018. Accessed 20 Dec. 2019. https://time.com/5482144/christmas-wreath-origins/

From Bauhaus to the Well-Centered Home

...continued

modernist architecture. Founded in 1919 in Germany, the Bauhaus was forced out by the Nazis in 1933, accelerating its influence and machine aesthetic throughout the world of art and architecture. Its leader, Walter Gropius, famously lived by the rule "Less is more."

There is some wisdom in that statement when referring to the removal of clutter and superfluous ornament. But when "less is more" devolves into the omission of human emotion, and architecture descends into a cold world of Spartan interiors and machine-made objects, I have no use for it.

Maybe it's because I also have a degree in psychology that I quickly grew tired of house designs that looked like museums and only begrudgingly allowed a couple of pieces of hard, angular, modernist furniture to be placed inside. In my view, architecture should offer a place for human beings to live and work that honors their connection to the natural world. It must respond to emotions and nurture a sense of well-being rather than merely being

continued on the next page...

From Bauhaus to the
Well-Centered Home

...continued

an assembly of geometrically arranged objects and bright, shiny materials.

My passion is designing homes, and that has been my specialty for the past three decades. I enjoy figuring out the reasons behind the forms and spaces, how they can nurture the emotional well-being of the people who live within, and how they can be beautiful. I create each new home from that understanding. I don't have a signature style, but I have had people say they can identify my homes by their feel.

This book and theory are the culmination of all my years of marrying architecture with psychology. The concept of the well-centered home brings together what I have learned about how we all are influenced by the built environment—and especially by our homes. The Bauhaus was wrong. More is more. The more well-centered our home is, the more mindful, balanced, and peaceful we become.

Solar Orienting

Once you have completed the anchoring and earth-grounding exercises outlined above, it's time to take advantage of what you've learned about your home's position in the universe. **Solar orienting** involves understanding the sun angles around your home at different times of the day and different seasons of the year and then harnessing that knowledge to make the most of natural daylight in your space.

The sun is the primary source of life on earth. It is nature's clock, and we should never underestimate its power as the basis for organizing our days. For example, consider the biannual anxiety of adjusting the clocks for Daylight Saving Time. Even this small change can wreak havoc on our biological clocks and is associated with increased automobile accidents.[3] But you can also arrange your home to take full advantage of the sun to create spaces that provide comfort at different times of the day or even different times of the year.

As an architect, solar orienting is a major part of my work. When I design a house, I take into account where the sun rises and sets, as well as the angle it will shine through

---

[3] Varughese, J. and Allen, R. P. "Fatal accidents following changes in daylight saving time: the American experience." *Sleep Med.* Jan. 2001. Accessed 20 Dec. 2019. https://www.ncbi.nlm.nih.gov/pubmed/?term=Varughese%20J%5BAuthor%5D&cauthor=true&cauthor_uid=11152980

the windows at different times of the year. My job is to make sure harsh afternoon light doesn't blast through the dining windows, overheat the room, and spoil dinner. I also love to create comfortable nooks in which to sip a coffee in the morning sun. I had a client once send me a note about a year after her house was complete. In it she said she remembered me telling her that, due to the orientation of the house and the way the roof overhangs were designed, a particular corner of the great room would be in a nice warm sunbeam on a chilly day. Her letter was proof, as she wrote it from her chair in that very spot on a January morning.

You don't have to build your home from the ground up to take advantage of solar orienting. In your anchoring exercise, you learned to point in each of the four cardinal directions—north, south, east, and west—in your home. Now you know where to find morning sun (in rooms with east-facing windows), so you can create a seating area there, if possible, to help energize you as you prepare to face the day. (For many people, morning light can be an essential component of good mental health as it has been proven to effectively treat Seasonal Affective Disorder, commonly known as the winter blues.)[4] By understanding the angles of the sun throughout the day, you can also block out

---

[4] Miller, Michael Craig, MD. "Seasonal affective disorder: bring on the light." *Harvard Health Publishing*. 29 Oct. 2015. Accessed 20 Dec. 2019. https://www.health.harvard.edu/blog/seasonal-affective-disorder-bring-on-the-light-201212215663

intense afternoon sun to create cool, restful spaces throughout your home.

Quick Tip

Not surprisingly, solar orienting is a high priority for Galileo homebody types. Try adding a sundial to the patio or garden to connect to daily solar cycles. This can be a fun, low-cost enhancement for everyone, but Galileos will especially enjoy keeping time by the sun.

LUNAR ORIENTING

Just as solar orienting helps you work with the natural cycles of the sun in your home, **lunar orienting** takes the moon's position into account. Human beings have always been fascinated by the moon, connecting it to both love and lunacy in our lore. It's a somewhat mysterious force that inspires songs, controls the ebb and flow of the tides, and is believed by many to influence unusual behavior. If you've ever said, "Must be a full moon!" to explain a rash of unusual behavior, you've participated in our unique relationship to this particular satellite. Scientists have even begun to explore the moon's effect on mood in psychological studies and have found a connection between the cycles of the moon and bipolar patients' mood swings.[5] While it's

[5] Wehr, T. A. "Bipolar mood cycles and lunar tide cycles." *Molecular Psychiatry.* Apr. 2018. Accessed 20 Jan. 2020 at https://www.ncbi.nlm. nih.gov/pmc/articles/PMC5524624/

not entirely clear how or to what extent the moon affects behavior, I am certain that the moon—and in particular, a charming view of it—influences our emotions.

While solar orienting will affect your comfort every day, lunar orienting is the icing on the cake of a well-centered home. Watching the rise of a full moon is something truly special, partly because it only happens about once each month. But if you can take advantage of an east-facing window that lets the silvery glow of the rising moon enter your home, you'll regularly enjoy its magic and mystery in your life—truly, an experience worth creating in your home if you can.

PUTTING THEORY INTO PRACTICE: TIPS FOR GETTING GROUNDED

No matter where you live—whether you rent or own, have a tiny studio or a five-bedroom expanse—you can take meaningful steps towards anchoring and earth-grounding in your home. Many of these techniques are quick and temporary, which makes them perfect for apartments where you may not have permission to alter the structure of the space. Because budgets are always a consideration, I've divided these ideas into categories based on relative cost. Not every idea will resonate with every person, and that's just fine: a big part of anchoring is making your place in the universe one of a kind.

$($S$)$ Getting Started with Limited Funds

- **Remove clutter from the exterior of the house.** Clutter disrupts the flow of energy, so rake leaves, get rid of broken toys, and remove any trash that's been piling up. Clutter is an interference that makes it harder to connect to your personal space.

- **Remove screens seasonally.** Window screens block 10 to 15 percent of daylight and blur the view. Take them down in the fall to enjoy more sun. If you have windows you never open, get rid of the screens permanently for year-round sunshine.

- **Keep windows clean and clear.** Clean glass has an enormous impact on your view. Remove heavy drapes or open them as wide as you can, then get busy with the window cleaner for easy, effective earth-grounding. This is especially important for east-facing windows that provide views of the sun and moon as they rise.

- **Add a framed map to your decor.** A historical or surveyor's map of your neighborhood is a great conversation piece and provides a reminder of your position in the world. Hang it where you want to feel reassured and comforted.

- **Design seating areas around local landmarks.** If you can see something from your living room window that makes your property or neighborhood unique, rearrange the furniture so everyone can enjoy that view, whether it's the Empire State Building, a church steeple, or a nearby mountain.

- **When you don't have a view, add artwork.** Pieces made from stone or artwork depicting rocky cliffs are excellent for anchoring because they enhance the impression of solid foundation, but all nature scenes will improve earth-grounding. Likewise, you can provide a "view" in all four directions if you add mirrors or pictures of nature as a substitute for a missing window.

- **Add houseplants.** A bit of living greenery is ideal for earth-grounding—just make sure you keep it alive. A dead plant blocks positive energy and wreaks havoc on the well-centered home.

- **Place a birdfeeder near a window where you spend time.** This simple addition invites living creatures to flit into view regularly. Their sounds and motions amplify the earth-grounding effect. Place it where you will look at it often—and where you won't forget to keep it filled with seed.

$ $ Investing in the Future

- **Repair exterior surfaces as needed.** Peeling paint, rotting siding, and broken concrete paths all take away from the feeling of stability and permanence that you need in order to feel your home is securely anchored.

- **Replace lightweight doors with sturdier options.** Hollow-core doors and flimsy bi-folds don't have the weight required to make your house feel like a safe, permanent structure. In particular, a front entry made of stained wood is more expressive of security than a painted door, and the visible wood grain enhances earth-grounding by connecting you to natural materials.

- **Trim hedges and vegetation that block your view.** Overgrown foundation plantings block the light and your view of the world around you, which makes it hard to feel anchored. Prune foundation shrubbery to a point below the windowsills. Cut back or remove overgrown trees and bushes that are interfering with solar orienting.

- **Install a compass rose inlay.** This is an excellent addition to a foyer floor, or perhaps a patio area you pass often as you enter your home. Make sure it is properly positioned so the arrow points north, and you'll always be anchored.

- **Add stone for a sense of weight.** Fireplaces, countertops, and floors are all opportunities to incorporate natural stone for more anchoring in your decor.

- **Replace carpet with hardwood flooring.** Wood is one of the finest materials for earth-grounding, and having it under your feet will connect you to nature with every step. Viewing the grain of the wood subconsciously links you to the living origin of the material.

- **Add glass patio doors.** If you can replace windows with French or sliding doors to connect to an outdoor living space, do it. Even if you rarely use them, the knowledge that you could step into nature whenever you wish is powerful. It lets your awareness "step outside" even when you do not do so physically.

- **Replace wooden decks with masonry.** Adding stone to enhance an entry deck or other transition to an outdoor living space will provide visual weight and a strong connection to the natural world.

- **Install a skylight.** Adding a skylight helps bring natural daylight into dim rooms, which enhances your feeling of well-being as well as the appearance of your home. Properly positioned skylights also enhance solar and lunar orienting.

$ $ $ Making Major Changes

- **Replace skimpy interior trim.** Narrow door casings, baseboards, window trim, and crown moulding all feel less permanent than wider options with more interesting profiles. Replacing the trim can add character and substance to your home without a full remodel.

- **Landscape for views.** If you don't like what you see out your window, change it! Planting a tree or a perennial garden to be viewed from the room where you spend the most time will vastly improve your sense of being earth-grounded.

- **Remove structures that interfere with your view.** A garage that blocks the moonrise or a privacy fence that hides a vernal pond might be wish-list items, but if it's within your power and budget to redesign these features for better earth-grounding, do it!

- **Build out walls to appear thicker.** Adding a wall of shelves and window seats can create the illusion of thicker walls. Doing this enhances the sense of the home being secure and immovable in a storm.

- **Add a water feature outdoors.** A fountain or naturalistic waterfall does wonders for earth-grounding, especially if you design it so the water flows toward the house. You want to send all the positive energy toward your living space.

- **Add stone walls and terraces.** These work best when connected directly to the house. Using stone to build substantial spaces in your landscape grounds your home to the earth and anchors it in place. It increases the impression that the house is linked to the earth and grew up from it.

- **Add a screened porch or sunroom.** Creating rooms that allow you to be surrounded by nature on three sides is a wonderful way to connect with the cycles of the sun, moon, and seasons.

- **Create a reflecting pool in your garden.** Positioned well, a reflecting pool will allow you to view the sun and the moon from the comfort of your home—ideal for staying connected with them all winter long.

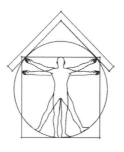

Chapter 4

REMOVING PEBBLES IN THE SHOE: SMALL ADJUSTMENTS THAT MAKE A HUGE DIFFERENCE

O nce you've begun to appreciate your home's place in the universe, you're ready to begin the real work of centering. This journey starts not by adding new furniture or applying a new coat of paint, but by taking stock of what you have and removing irritants that get in your way, so you're able to relax and enjoy your space.

Things in your home that are working against you and are disrupting your home's beneficial energy are like a pebble in your shoe. You may go out and buy yourself a wonderful new outfit and fix your hair so you're looking good, but none of those things will remove the pain of walking with a pebble in your shoe. No matter how many positive things you add, they won't remove that irritant. In this way, a negative influence can be stronger than a positive one. Removing the negatives is its own job, and one that should be done before you begin to add things to your home.

My wife and I enjoy spending the winter at a vacation cottage in South Carolina. We acquired an existing home that was fully furnished, so our first centering tasks have been to remove the pebbles that have been rubbing us the wrong way in this space. For example, the original living room furniture arrangement was awkward at best, with a split focus between the television and fireplace and no place to hold a conversation. We rearranged the furniture several times and finally found an arrangement where, once it was in place, we said, "Ah! This is better."

As we worked to remove this particular pebble in the living room, we noticed a new irritant. Sitting in the living room, guests can look in one direction and see directly into a bathroom. To me, that is a conflict of major proportions: a view of the toilet feels out of place when I'm trying to relax with friends and family. It finally occurred to me that I could change the swing of the door. I moved the hinges from the left side to the right side of the door, and now the door blocks the view of the plumbing fixtures, even when it is partially open. This was a pretty simple fix, and certainly less expensive than redesigning the layout of the first floor.

Many changes that remove negative energy are simple and inexpensive, though adjustments can be bigger. For example, you may have a tiny window that offers just a peek at a beautiful view, and every time you pass it, you wish you could be more connected to that outdoor space. Or you may have an awkward path of travel between rooms that makes it hard to serve your guests in your dining room. Tearing down walls and reworking floor plans are other ways to remove pebbles—especially when those pebbles have been so bothersome that they feel more like boulders blocking you from enjoying your home.

Quick Tip

Remove furnishings and accessories that cramp your space or create a feeling of stuffiness. Astaire homebody types need room for guests to mix and mingle freely.

PEBBLES ARE PERSONAL

Of course, what bothers one person may not affect another. If you'd been a guest in my home, you might never have overtly noticed the view of the bathroom from the living room, even though it was a constant irritation for me. However, these kinds of conflicts and discords are pebbles that have an undeniable subliminal negative impact on each of us. Most people are affected by sensory stimuli that encroach upon an otherwise harmonious space. Irritants may be visual, as in my examples above, but they may also be auditory, tactile, or even olfactory.

Part of the work of centering, then, is learning to fine-tune your senses to pay closer attention to the stimuli that surround you. As you sit in your chair right now, what do you see around you? How does the quality of light make you feel? Do you feel a sense of spaciousness, or are things cluttered and cramped?

Next, shift your attention to your other senses. What do you hear in this room? Is there the rumble of traffic, or a noisy appliance? Birdsong or rustling leaves? Do smells waft in on the air? If so, are they pleasant? How does the floor feel under your feet? What textures brush against your skin? Do you find the temperature comfortable?

Human beings are adaptive creatures, so it's easy to become accustomed to the quality of your environment. That's why, when people put a house up for sale, they end up correcting many problems they'd stopped noticing. Suddenly, that squeaky door or peeling paint is of prime importance—and all because you turned your attention to something that had been interfering with your psychological balance and ability to relax all along.

Quick Tip

Remove kitsch and clutter. Galileo homebody types have no interest in objects that simply take up space without being useful or thought-provoking.

The Vastu Method for Homes of Positive Energy

Vastu shastra is a traditional Indian system of architectural planning designed to bring positive energy into the home. Like feng shui, vastu utilizes a mapping diagram to determine which spaces are auspicious for certain functions and uses. The diagram is intricate, with nine primary squares each divided into nine secondary squares for a total of 81 squares—each with its own characteristics. As you can imagine, the potential for mistakes or "pebbles" within this system is high indeed!

The home is laid out based on the dictates of the grid. A vastu home must be perfectly oriented to the points of the compass; for example, the front door must be located in a particular secondary square and open to the east. The central primary square is called the *Brahmastan* and must be open to the sky. Staircases must only turn clockwise as they ascend and consist of an odd number of steps. There are requirements for points where light must be able to pass through the entire house, a prescribed square for cooking, locations where toilets must not be, and many, many more dictates that must be honored.

continued on the next page...

> ### The Vastu Method for Homes of Positive Energy
>
> ...continued
>
> When the guidelines and rules are followed *and* the vastu home is designed specifically for its occupants, the home radiates positive energy, and the people dwelling within come under the healing and positive influence of its energy field. It's no easy feat, but the results can be incredibly soothing.

SEEING YOUR HOME IN A NEW LIGHT

Some pebbles are easy to identify—almost everyone has a mental list of things in their home that they would like to change. But others tend to hover under our everyday radar until something (often a real estate agent) calls attention to them.

The trick, then, is to improve your sensitivity to the energy in your home. One way to do this is to photograph your home *as if* you were posting photos for a real estate listing. This shift in perspective—from contented occupant to skeptical potential buyer—will help you see your home with new eyes.

So grab your smartphone and start taking photos of each room from as many angles as you can. Then, look at the photos as if you were seeing your home for the first time.

Do you have the right lighting? Are things in the right place? The photos will help you get out of your normal viewpoint, heighten your awareness, and focus in a way that you wouldn't on an ordinary day.

 **Quick Tip**

Sharp or potentially dangerous objects are pebbles that cause worry for Nightingale homebody types. You'll be happier without these anxiety-producing items.

COMMON PEBBLES IN EACH ROOM OF THE HOME

As you study your photos of each room, you're sure to see plenty of pebbles that are unique to your home—or to your personality and levels of sensitivity. But there are also common irritants that add negative energy to any home where they are found.

To help improve your perception as you search for pebbles, I've created a checklist of items that everyone should remove from their homes. These are the most common irritants that I've come across in my years of work in people's homes, and removing or correcting them *always* makes a difference—even if you hadn't noticed them before.

Across the Whole House

- Replace burned-out light bulbs.

- Replace too-dim light bulbs with brighter ones.

- Replace lampshades to reduce glare or allow more light to shine through.

- Seal doors and windows against drafts.

- Oil squeaky door hinges.

- Repair faulty door handles, latches, and locks.

- Adjust crooked pictures on the wall.

- Assess window treatments to make sure they don't block desirable views.

- Get rid of dying or neglected houseplants. It's better not to have them at all than to invite the negative energy that comes from neglect—a condition I'll talk about in more detail in Chapter 5.

- Remove clutter and things that are out of place. If this feels overwhelming, don't worry—I'll provide much more detail about how to accomplish this in Chapter 7.

Living Room

- Experiment with furniture arrangement to promote conversation and comfort.

- Evaluate the sight lines from every seat in the living room to make sure they don't point toward undesirable views or away from points of interest.

- Find a better position for any chairs with their backs toward the main entrance to the room. People subconsciously feel insecure in this position, because there's the chance someone could sneak up behind them.

Kitchen/Dining Room

- Fix noisy appliances. This can often be accomplished by making sure they're level and that all parts are securely attached.

- Make sure all cabinet doors and drawers function properly. Oil drawer glides and replace missing handles as needed.

- Remove clutter from countertops. While it's fine to have useful appliances out in the open, it's best to put away things that are used less often to free up counter space and reduce visual chaos.

- Clean the oven and refrigerator. These are common irritants that we tend to ignore because they don't get dirty overnight. An oven with a clean window through which you can observe your food and a refrigerator that's neatly organized will make you feel much better about cooking.

- Clear the dining table and kitchen island of remnants of other activities before eating.

Study or Office

- Remove clutter from your desk or worktable. When items stack up, it makes it hard to concentrate and use your space as designed.

- Make sure your work area is isolated from other parts of the home as much as possible. This may involve rearranging furniture to block distracting views and sounds.

Bedroom

- Consider soundproofing walls that border common areas, such as a bathroom or den. This can be a big project, but the results are well worth it.

- Remove harsh lighting inside and out. This may mean adjusting window treatments to block a streetlamp or replacing harsh overhead lights with gentle lamps for your bedside table.

- Don't leave clothing lying on the floor. If this is a habit, you may need a larger hamper or additional closet hooks to hold items as you dress for bed.

Bathroom

- Consider ways to block the view of the toilet from outside the bathroom. Many master bathrooms are now designed with a separate closet for the toilet, but adjusting the swing of the door or strategically placing a screening element may also help.

- Cleanliness is key. In addition to basic cleaning, remove any rust or water stains from fixtures. Shine up the mirror and faucets regularly.

- Address any leaks or drips. It's often quite simple to tighten a faucet or adjust the ballcock assembly to keep a toilet from running, which will eliminate irritating sounds and conserve water.

Patio or Porch

- Sweep and power-wash the driveway and paths for a more pleasant transition into the home.

- Clear away fallen leaves and twigs.

- Address landscaping problems that prevent water from draining away from the house. Puddles in your path are major irritants and lead to you tracking more dirt and debris into the home as well.

- Repair or replace severely cracked walkways and driveways.

- Remove dirt, debris, and spider webs that tend to build up in corners.

- Keep furniture and other items stored neatly in the off-season, especially if you have windows that provide a view of the porch or patio.

 Quick Tip

Get rid of objects that are mass-produced or poorly made. Plato homebody types value craftsmanship but dislike visual clutter, so eliminate inferior items first.

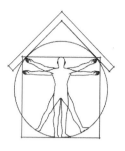

Chapter 5

PEOPLING THE SPACE: MAKING YOUR HOME MORE HUMAN

As I've mentioned before, centering the home is all about creating balance. It's no surprise, then, that the process of centering and the work you do to harness your home's energy also require balance. In the previous chapter, you learned how to remove pebbles to help eliminate negative energy. In this chapter, we'll begin to balance those removals with some additions that will increase the positive energy in your home.

I call these positive additions *pearls*. When an oyster is confronted with an irritating grain of sand—a pebble in its shoe, if you will—it has a unique way of solving that problem. The oyster coats the pebble with layers of nacre, the same substance that makes up its protective shell. The oyster transforms its irritation into something that is not only less irritating, but also beautiful. This is what we want to do as we center our homes: we remove the pebbles that irritate us and add pearls that bring pleasure.

One of the most fundamental additions to any home is people. Your home is a space designed for people to eat, sleep, create, nurture relationships, and engage in all the other activities that make up a full life. This requires creating a space that's designed for humans—what I call *peopling the space*.

In architectural terms, peopling is the process of defining the scale of the space and giving it characteristics that imply that people have occupied that space in the past and will continue to do so in the future. Peopling means setting up a space—in this case, your home—to express that it is for people to interact in.

Peopling the space adds greatly to our comfort in buildings. If you were to walk into a warehouse, it clearly wouldn't feel like a space for people. It's a big, open box that will create the same type of discomfort as that empty basketball arena we discussed in Chapter 1—not a comfortable place to sit and relax. The warehouse is missing two things: features that bring it down to an appropriate human size, and objects that create the sense that people belong there.

Residential architecture automatically does a better job than commercial warehouses in this regard, but there's still quite a bit you can do to fine-tune the energy in your home to resonate with the human beings who will spend time there.

SCALE AND THE GOLDILOCKS EFFECT

Scale is a term that architects throw around a lot, and it has to do with getting things the right size. The right size isn't just physical, however. It also has to do with the psychology of the space. Because we've been taught to think in terms of only five senses, many people have trouble articulating their sense of scale. In this way, we're like Goldilocks wandering through the three bears' home: We sense when a space is too big, too small, or just right.

For example, many people are beginning to realize that double-height ceilings in great rooms and family rooms just don't feel good. This was—and still is—an enormously popular trend in new home design, but as people have been living in these spaces, they have begun to see the many faults of the tall great room.

From a practical standpoint, sound echoes and bounces up into those high ceilings over balconies in ways that amplify it throughout the rest of the house. These rooms are also hard to light because the ceilings are so high. And forget changing the light bulbs. But they also just tend to feel cold and uncomfortable because they create a bit of that feeling of sitting in an empty stadium. The square footage of the room itself might not be that large, but the high ceilings and unbridled openness make it feel too big to enjoy intimate conversation or offer a cozy place to curl up with a book.

Architects bring too-large rooms down to size by defining the edges of the space. The most obvious way to define a space is by adding walls or a ceiling. This is the process by which the basic box of your home is defined and divided into areas for eating, resting, working, and entertaining. Other tools we use to define spaces are changes in ceiling height, and the addition of beams and columns that indicate you are psychologically moving from one area to another, even if there are no walls nearby. These are major space definers that are best addressed in the original design of the home, though they can be added in a remodel.

But there are also other, less labor-intensive ways to indicate edges to define a space. We do this by drawing lines that trick the eye into marking the edge of a space. For example, an open concept area that holds both the living area and the dining area can easily be divided by putting down two area rugs. These immediately outline a spot for the table and a spot for the sofa, and your eyes are telling your brain that there are two comfortable "rooms" here instead of one big one.

Adding trim and other woodwork is another time-honored way to draw a line around certain spaces in your home. For example, those double-height ceilings can be addressed by installing a cornice or line of moulding around the room at a height of nine to ten feet. This is a traditional architectural technique that stops the eye and tells your brain that the room ends there, even though the ceiling is actually much higher. You can strengthen this effect by painting the portion of the wall above the cornice the same color as the ceiling.

Likewise, a chandelier or other hanging light fixture will help bring a cavernous room down to a more livable scale by putting a "lid" on the room. Many people hang these too close to the ceiling in double-height great rooms and foyers, but the body of the light fixture should be low enough to hover at that nine- to ten-foot cornice line to create the implication of a lower ceiling.

Of course, not everything Goldilocks tried was too big. Sometimes our sense of scale is out of balance in the other direction, causing us to feel cramped and hemmed in by spaces that feel too small. Homeowners with enough time and resources can add larger windows or increase the square footage of rooms to provide more space—sometimes the addition of just a few feet is enough to make room for a comfortable conversation area or dining nook that makes a huge difference.

But there are other ways to work with scale that don't require a major renovation. Instead of defining the edges to stop the eye, there are a few tricks that will blur the edges and make it hard to tell exactly where your room ends. These types of tricks make your brain assume a space is larger than it really is.

Most people have heard that dark-colored walls make a room look smaller, but the opposite is actually true— provided the room has adequate lighting to make up for the fact that dark surfaces are less reflective. A dark-colored wall makes it hard for your eye and brain to detect how far away it is. To appreciate this effect, take a look at a window that sits in a dark-painted wall. See if you don't agree that the window will seem to almost float in the wall because the wall's location has become difficult to judge accurately. You don't have to commit to a darker color for the whole room, either. Even a single accent wall in a dark color will perceptually push that wall out to an undefined location and make the room feel bigger.

Mirrors are another effective way to fool the eye into thinking a room is larger than it is. A full-mirrored wall can be very effective, but you can also add a framed mirror anywhere you wish you had a window to visually remove that portion of the wall and add the illusion of space. I have seen actual windows installed in interior walls and mirrors were inserted in place of the transparent glass. The effect of opening up that side of the room was impressive and improved the feel of the room. Mirrors are wonderful pearls to add to any room that is not well earth-grounded or feels too enclosed.

In my own home, an older home we bought and added on to, I had to adjust the scale of the eight-foot ceilings in the existing part of the house—the opposite of the great room problem discussed above. These ceilings are a bit too low for comfort by today's standards and created a feeling of being boxed in. I solved this by painting the ceilings light blue. This hinders the eye's ability to measure the distance of the ceiling from the floor, because as human beings we are programmed to have light blue above us. Subconsciously we know that the sky is very far away, so a blue ceiling tricks us into feeling there is open sky above us. We painted all our ceilings blue at home, and guests don't even notice the color unless we mention it—they just know they feel comfortable in a right-sized space. That's the power of working with scale to channel energy in your home.

(S) Quick Tip

Painting your ceilings is an inexpensive way to add a feeling of spaciousness to your home. My color of choice for blue ceilings is Benjamin Moore's Buxton Blue (BM HC-149), a pale blue with a very faint undertone of green that mutes the harshness of a pure light blue.

Haint Blue and Its Paranormal Origin

"Haint Blue" is the traditional color of porch ceilings in the American South. This tradition originated with the Gullahs, enslaved African-Americans who lived and worked on the indigo plantations in the Low Country and islands of South Carolina, Georgia, and Florida.

Haint Blue is a pale blue, made from a pigment originally derived from the local indigo plants. The color was purported to have mystical powers to keep away evil spirits known as haunts or, in the unique Gullah dialect, "haints." Some legends have it that this hue fooled the haints into thinking the porch ceiling was the sky, tricking them into flying through it. Other stories say that the ghosts thought the porch ceilings were water, which haints traditionally could not cross.

My own porch ceilings are painted Haint Blue, along with the ceilings inside my house. The result? I have no haints or ghosts in or around my house. It must work!

HUMAN HANDS CREATE A HOME

Achieving appropriate scale is only half the work of peopling a space. You also need to add elements to your home that highlight the fact that people belong there.

You automatically have many things at human scale in a house, but it's also important to understand the principle of maintenance as it relates to the energy in your home.

Objects that require maintenance have the psychological effect of connecting you with the person who does the maintenance (even if that person is you). For example, consider silverware that needs to be polished, plants that need to be watered and pruned, or a clock that needs to be wound. These items cannot exist in their ideal states without a human hand coming in contact with them. Therefore, items that require maintenance gain another level of energy or influence on our psyches.

Of course, anything that requires maintenance must actually *be maintained*: Dead plants and clocks with dead batteries that are stopped or display the wrong time are pebbles that should be avoided. The trick is to know yourself and choose elements that you'll enjoy maintaining, so you keep up with them. In this way, pebbles that bring negative energy into your home can be transformed into pearls that bring joy—all with just a few moments of dedication to their upkeep.

Have you ever wondered why most people prefer handmade objects over machine-made objects, even though the handmade objects are likely to be less perfect than the machine-made ones? It's possible to suggest the presence of a human hand by choosing decorative items that required human contact to create them in the first place. Handmade objects prompt your subconscious mind to envision the effort it took to craft the piece, which subtly connects you to another human being across space and time. Pottery, wood carvings, blown glass, and woven textiles are all wonderful examples of items that people the space by showing the hand of the maker at work. Reclaimed wooden beams are also a nice connector because they had a previous life—someone cut the tree, shaped the beams, and lived under their shelter for many years before they were lovingly installed in your home.

For people who live alone, it's especially important to people the space with items that suggest human connection. You might live by yourself, but creating places for another person to join you creates a more comfortable environment, even when you aren't hosting anyone. There's an old Southern tradition of setting an extra place at the table for the possibility of an unexpected guest arriving at dinnertime. To people the space, arrange your house with that same philosophy of hospitality in mind. Have a dining area with space for at least one or two other people to join you for a meal, and arrange your living room furniture in a seating group that is designed for conversation. A pair of chairs angled slightly toward each other will feel more comfortable than a single chair facing a television, even in a studio apartment for one. A properly peopled space keeps you company by suggesting the presence of others.

 **Quick Tip**

Astaire homebody types are such social creatures that they may need more overt peopling to feel at home in a space. To meet this need, choose artwork that depicts groups of people, especially scenes of people performing for or interacting with others.

The Power of Columns as Human Forms

As humans, we tend to anthropomorphize objects; that is, we subconsciously see them as people. If you've ever seen a "face" in a car by seeing its headlights as eyes and the grill as its mouth, that's your anthropomorphizing brain at work.

In architecture, columns are forms that echo the tall, slender torsos of humans when scaled to do so. At the University of Virginia, there is a central area called The Lawn, which is surrounded by columns. You can never feel alone on The Lawn surrounded by these human-sized forms. Instead, you feel surrounded by friends, even when you're alone.

Inside the home, rounded columns are especially effective for peopling. Not only do

continued on the next page...

> ### The Power of Columns as Human Forms
>
> **...continued**
>
> they add a human element, but they also help divide and define the spaces. This is why many homes use a pair of columns in the woodwork to help divide the living area from the dining room—it's peopling the space on a number of levels.

TIPS FOR PEOPLING YOUR SPACE

As with so many aspects of the centering process, peopling your space requires heightening your awareness of your surroundings so you can become more sensitive to the energy coursing through your home. The best way to become more attuned to the energy provided by human hands is to "proofread" your space.

In writing, we often focus on the big concepts and ideas first, but at some point a writer must comb through the manuscript word by word to check for spelling and punctuation errors. Similarly, you can "proofread" your home by taking the time to look at each individual object in a room. Take a moment to behold the item and consider how it was made. Was it stamped out in a factory, or does it reflect the work of an artisan? Do you have to maintain it in some way, and if you do, does that feel inspiring or onerous?

Once you've considered objects one by one, you can decide how they contribute to the overall balance of human energy in your home. This exercise will help you tune in to the ways you've already peopled your space, and you will discover whether you need to subtract any pebbles, add more pearls, or better define the edges of your space to bring it into scale.

As you begin to proofread, keep these tips in mind for making adjustments that will help you people your space:

- **Hang artwork at eye level.** Generally speaking, the center of your painting or grouping of wall art should be about five feet off the ground. This subtly reminds the viewer that the artwork is hung with a human observer in mind.

- **Add lines to visually define your space.** Trim moulding, such as cornices and chair rails, is very effective in this regard. You may also consider adding grids that help the eye measure the space. Windows with divided lights—i.e., windows with slender bars called muntins dividing the panes of glass—are a traditional way to do this.

- **Choose hardware with your hand in mind.** While geometric shapes may be visually interesting, they do not fit comfortably in the hand and become a tactile pebble. Rounded doorknobs and drawer pulls that are the right size for your hand are a much better choice.

- **Choose furniture that's in scale with your body.** Oversized furniture looks nice in photos, but it's hard to work with. If you're short, don't choose furniture that allows your feet to dangle when seated or a bed that forces you to climb up into it. This is not a one-size-fits-all concept. Comfort is key.

- **Respect your personal space parameters.** We all have a feel for the space that "belongs" to us and how much distance we need from others to feel comfortable. The distances you allow between seats and other objects must be responsive to your need for personal space. Too far away, and you'll lose connectivity. Too close, and you'll feel invaded. Always test your furniture arrangements to see how they feel in practice.

- **Invite animals into your space.** Pets may be the ultimate indicator of maintenance and are a wonderful way to people the space—but only if they'll make you happy. You might also consider artwork depicting animals to draw upon our natural tendency toward anthropomorphism.

Quick Tip

Plato homebody types are particularly interested in objects with an interesting history behind them. When choosing objects to people the space, search for handmade crafts that are also antiques to provide fascinating focal points.

Sixteen Items with Extra Peopling Power

Anything handmade or requiring maintenance will help you people your space, but some objects provide more of this energy than others. Some top choices for instant peopling:

1. Aquarium with fish

2. Bonsai trees

3. Tabletop Zen garden

4. Original artwork

5. Reclaimed wood

6. Reclaimed bricks

7. Quilts

8. Pottery

9. Portraits

continued on the next page...

Sixteen Items with Extra Peopling Power

...continued

10. Fresh flowers

11. Stained glass

12. Stitchery and needlework

13. Sculpture

14. Carved wooden pieces

15. Hand-painted tiles

16. Books

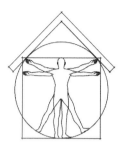

Chapter 6

SEQUENTIAL PROGRESSIONS: OUTDOOR TO INDOOR, PUBLIC TO PRIVATE, GROUP TO SOLITARY

Though your house itself doesn't move through space, you will spend a good deal of time moving within your home. As you move from one place to another, the transitions should feel smooth, not jarring. This will allow you to flow *with* the energy in your home rather than feel like you are fighting against it.

To accomplish these soothing transitions, you'll need to create *progressions*—intermediate steps along the way from one aspect to another. I liken progressions to shifting gears while driving. You wouldn't want to shift from drive to reverse without first shifting into neutral—you'd strip out the gears.

Your home is a little like that. You don't want to experience an abrupt, jarring change that causes discomfort. For example, if you came immediately from the outdoors into a bedroom at the main entrance, you would feel disoriented. (This example may sound extreme, but I have seen it—and corrected it—in my work as an architect.) Adding progressions means that you create some intermediate space along the way to help your subconscious mind ease out of one space and into another. Softening the transition keeps you from getting knocked off balance and preserves the quality of spaces so they don't bleed confusingly into each other.

There are three important progressions that occur in every home, no matter its size or location. These are progressions from the indoors to the outdoors, from public to private spaces, and from group interactions to solitary contemplation. Understanding how to work with each of these progressions will help you achieve that most elusive of feelings in your home: *flow*.

Flow is one of those terms that we instinctively understand but have trouble articulating—you know it when you feel it. By sensitizing yourself to the progressions in your home, you'll cultivate a deeper understanding of flow and be able to create it more purposefully as you continue centering your living space.

Outdoor to Indoor Progressions

Outdoor to indoor transitions are the most obvious shifts that occur in your home. It's very easy to mark where these changes happen, because the transition point is clearly defined by walls and a door. The exterior is 100 percent outdoor space, while the interior is 100 percent indoor space.

Creating successful progressions requires you to find ways to ease the transition between two different areas. In this case, you're looking to create an intermediate space that creates the feel of being more 50/50—that is, partially outdoors and partially indoors at the same time.

Now, it's technically not possible to be in between the outdoors and the indoors, except perhaps right on the threshold of your front door. Progressions are an artful way of suggesting an in-between to your mind's eye. To do this, we use objects as focal points that command and define space in a different way. These space definers can be walls, half walls, other architectural elements, or decor items like plants or a screen—anything that serves to mark where one space ends and another begins.

To understand how objects define spaces, imagine yourself in the middle of a grassy meadow with a solitary tree. If you were planning a picnic, you would inevitably find yourself spreading out your blanket somewhere near that tree and not out in the undefined open space of the meadow. That's about more than just finding shade on a sunny day. Subconsciously, you want to be in the space that is dominated by that tree. As we learned in Chapter 5, it's more comforting to be in a space that is clearly defined than somewhere that's limitless and not scaled for people. Our inner selves are not happy when they are disconnected and adrift.

Creating progressions, then, is about using objects in a thoughtful way to define intermediate "connector" spaces. To see how it works for outdoor to indoor transitions, imagine a townhome or apartment building with a series of front doors along a walkway. Virtually none of the outdoor space is claimed by the homes behind the doors. But the simple act of adding a doormat will define the space in front of the door and let passersby know that there's something waiting inside. That subtle hint claims the space and has turned it from a 100 percent outdoor space to a 95 percent outdoor space, with the doormat serving as a little bit of the indoors outside.

To build a stronger progression, add a shrub or two to the landscaping or some potted plants along the walkway, and you've made a real statement about where that space belongs—you've claimed it as part of the indoor space. It's now something like 80 percent outdoor and 20 percent indoor, or part of your home.

The next step is to walk through that door and into a foyer, rather than directly into a living space. The foyer is a transitional area that is perhaps 25 percent outdoor and

75 percent indoor. It is technically inside the shelter of your house, but it's not a place where you would stop to rest for any extended period. You might have weatherproof flooring, a coatrack, and an umbrella stand here, all of which indicate that you're not completely indoors—from an emotional standpoint, at least.

In this way, a foyer is a classic marker of the outdoor-to-indoor progression. It's popular for its practicality, of course, but it also offers the mind a smooth transition from one world to another. If you don't have a foyer in your home or apartment, it's crucial to create at least a small "landing pad" that functions this way. This is easily done by adding a bit of tile or flagstone flooring to the area just inside your exterior door.

You can also consider adding a coat tree or console table to keep outdoor items organized. In a very tiny space, even a shelf where you can keep your keys or the dog's leash will make a difference. These additions don't just keep your entryway uncluttered. They also provide a place where you subconsciously leave behind the cares of the day before you fully enter your home's inner sanctuary. They help you come in for a soft landing and set you on the path toward mindfulness and self-centering.

ⓢ ⓢ ⓢ Quick Tip

If your budget and city ordinances allow, building a small addition to serve as the main entrance to your home is well worth the effort. A bump-out will provide space for a foyer or mudroom to serve as the ideal transition between indoor and outdoor spaces. Likewise, you could expand a stoop into a covered porch with room for seating to create a more pleasing progression.

PUBLIC TO PRIVATE PROGRESSIONS

There is some overlap between outdoor-to-indoor progressions and public-to-private progressions. In general, the outdoors is a public space and the indoors a private one, but it's not always a perfect correspondence. For example, an apartment balcony is an outdoor space, but one that is more private than public. It feels like an extension of your living room, so you treat it as part of your home. Likewise, an interior hallway or stairwell connecting apartments is an indoor space, but it feels more public than private. Therefore, public-to-private progressions have to do with the functions of spaces just as much as their physical locations. And to be clear, the word *public* has two meanings for me. On one hand it could mean the general public and on the other hand it could mean the other members of your family or guests in your house. Both definitions call for proper transitions from the public spaces to the private spaces.

To get a sense of how you progress from public to private spaces in your home, think of it as if it were a train. As the largest room in your house and a very common point of entry, the garage is the engine. From this first car on the train, you progress backward through a series of rooms that gradually move you from public to private spaces. From the garage you move into the kitchen. Like a coal car on the train, it should be near the engine so you don't have to go far for fuel (or to get groceries from your SUV to the fridge).

Next is the dining car, or your dining room, which of course must be located near the kitchen for convenience. A coach car would be next—a public space to sit, relax, and enjoy the ride. In the home, this corresponds to a living room or family room where people gather. Last on the line are the sleeping cars, which are your bedrooms. These are your private rooms.

If you imagine your home laid out in a logical line with connections from public rooms to private rooms like a train, it's easy to build a smooth progression from public to private spaces. In architecture, however, we don't design a home as a long line of rooms. We take those spaces and fold them up to fit in a more compact footprint—but the connections have to remain the same and do the job of easing the progression from public spaces to private spaces. For example, if your bedroom door opens directly to the kitchen, you have a very abrupt transition between public and private spaces, and that's going to feel uncomfortable for most people. That would be two train cars out of order.

The trick is to become attuned to how you use each room so you can ensure that you have comfortable progressions between public and private areas of the home. For example, many older homes have bathrooms positioned next to and accessible from the kitchen, but this is about as harsh a conflict as you can imagine in a house. Placing the part of the home where food is prepared next to the place where human waste is disposed of creates an extreme conflict in energy. And just from a practical viewpoint, privacy, sanitary considerations, and simple sensibilities demand that there should be a buffer between these two functions.

To create a bit of distance between the two, it's helpful to compel people to take a few extra steps or to change direction as they walk. These motions have the effect of lengthening the short time it takes to cross from one room into the next. If you can build a wall to screen the bathroom from the kitchen, or reconfigure the door to enter the bathroom at a different angle, you could lengthen the progression and create more psychological comfort here.

In two-story homes, the bedrooms are almost always upstairs, which is the ideal progression from public to private, as it takes a minute to move from one space to the next. In many one-story homes, bedrooms are separated from public areas by a short hallway. Sometimes, though, a bedroom might open directly onto the living room, and this creates considerable discomfort.

Fortunately, you can adjust this by arranging the bedroom furniture so that the bed is as far from the door as possible—ideally, not within sight from the living room. If that's not possible, a folding screen or artful arrangement of a dresser with a finished back could create a small vestibule inside the door to function the same way.

In all cases, the goal is to create some breathing room between public and private spaces to allow your mind to reset as you move from one to the other within your home.

⑤ ⑤ Quick Tip

Consider switching out pocket doors for hinged doors when space allows. Hinged doors can function as a visual shield that partially blocks your view of a private space. They operate almost silently and do a much better job keeping light, sound, and odors from moving from public to private spaces—and vice versa.

GROUP TO SOLITARY PROGRESSIONS

In her book *The Not So Big House: A Blueprint for the Way We Really Live*, architect and author Sarah Susanka discusses the concept of an "away room" as a crucial part of a house, no matter what its size.[6] For the purposes of discussing group to solitary progressions, I like to think in terms of an "away place" instead. It is an essential part of a well-centered home.

An office is one thing, but an away place could be a wingback chair where you can sit in pleasant isolation with

---

[6] Susanka, Sarah. *The Not So Big House: A Blueprint for the Way We Really Live*. Taunton, MA: The Taunton Press, 1998.

your thoughts. No matter where you place that chair, sitting in it signals to the family "I'm by myself right now"—even if you're in the middle of the living room. Every member of the household needs a place like that to function as a private zone.

In a very well designed house, there would be several areas that progress from group activities to solitary ones. In addition to a place for solitary contemplation, there should also be areas that encourage different levels of interaction. These could include a pair of chairs in the master bedroom for a couple to chat, an informal dining table for a family of four, and a large, formal dining area with seating for ten. Group-to-solitary progressions don't necessarily need to be directly linked to each other in sequential spaces, but they do need to exist in the home so there's always a comfortable spot to interact or to be alone.

Above all, your away place should support your personal preferences and homebody type to provide the ideal place to recharge your emotional batteries. At the outset of every design project, I encourage my clients to envision what their ideal place of solitude might be, considering all five senses. Once you fully understand that objective, you will see what you need to do to accomplish it.

For example, if you find yourself imagining a bright, sunny spot for your away place, then your first task is to look around your home to figure out where that place might be (and if you completed the exercises discussed in Chapter 3, you'll be able to identify the sunny spots with ease).

When choosing a spot for your away place, it's important to take into account what architects call the *circulation space* in your home. These are the areas where people pass through rooms and conduct most of their activity. It's helpful to envision the traffic patterns as a flowing stream. There are places in your home—hallways, for instance—that are main channels for motion, like the main channel of the stream. There are other spots that are eddying or quieting spaces, where there's less hustle and bustle. These are the small coves at the edges of the stream.

Use the quietest spots, the coves of the stream, for solitary spaces, and you'll create a pleasing progression that always feels right, whether you're alone or with others.

($) Quick Tip

In a very small home, a cozy chair is enough to create a meaningful away place. It doesn't even have to be separated from your conversational seating area. Lighting can enhance the separation, so add a side table and a reading lamp, and dim the lights in the rest of the room when you want to be alone with your thoughts.

Quick Tip

Nightingale homebody types respond to soft textiles and curved lines, so their away places should be outfitted with plush pillows and warm throw blankets to enhance comfort.

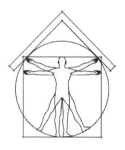

Chapter 7

A PLACE FOR EVERYTHING: WHY WE NEED ORDER, NOT CHAOS

We've discussed the flow of energy throughout the home in some detail, but another important aspect of centering has less to do with external forces than it does with what's going on inside your own mind. It's been well established in psychology that the human mind is always seeking to create order out of chaos. We do this during every moment of every day as we receive and respond to a constant barrage of sensory stimuli. As information comes in through our eyes, ears, noses, and skin, our brains automatically try to categorize it and file it in a place where it will help us understand our experiences.

From the day we are born, our brains begin to take in all that information and organize it into what psychologists call a *schema*. When we perceive our world, we are trying to understand it based on the many schemata we have already established in our minds. When we get new information that doesn't fit, our minds work overtime to put that chaos into some kind of new order.

Think of a schema as a drawer in your mental filing cabinet. A small child might have a whole filing cabinet for animals, with a drawer for "cats" and a drawer for "dogs," based on their first experiences with family pets. But suppose that child sees a cow for the first time. Where does it belong? She may initially call it a dog, but she'll eventually learn to create a whole new drawer—and so on for the entire animal kingdom.

Our brains are wonderfully complex, with an endless number of drawers that allow us to create schemata for all sorts of concepts. Each time we come upon something unfamiliar, there's a sense of discomfort until we can either file it into an existing schema or create a whole new schema to contain it. Like it or not, this is how we learn throughout our lives.

While this process is often an exciting part of being human, the feeling of discomfort that arises from confronting chaos and stimuli we cannot categorize is not always welcome. Most of the time, your brain does such a good job that you aren't aware of the process of creating new schemata. But sometimes the brain can become overwhelmed with the chaos of stimuli and act to shut it out. If you have ever felt like you've just had enough of dealing with the world and want to get away for a while, you understand this.

When your mind is busy working overtime to respond to excess stimuli—whether in the form of noise from the neighbors, clashing visual patterns, or a cluttered desk—it's very hard to relax. To center our homes, it is crucial to reduce the amount of stimuli we experience and give our minds a chance to sort everything out. When we create space for this process, we become more rested, more centered, and more mindful.

The Chinese Philosophy of Yin-Yang

While Western scholars are more comfortable with the science of psychology to explain our innate need for centering, Chinese culture addresses it in the philosophy of yin-yang. Yin and Yang are inseparable and contradictory opposites: light and dark, male and female, hot and cold. These forces pull in opposite directions and ideally reach a state of dynamic equilibrium in which they are in flux but largely balanced overall.

In Chinese mythology, Yin and Yang were born out of chaos at the dawn of the

continued on the next page...

The Chinese Philosophy of Yin-Yang

...continued

universe, but their balance at the center of things allowed for Pangu, the first human, to be born. Swirling around Pangu are the forces of the sun, moon, and tides, which are always changing but remain in balance.

In the home, Yin and Yang will feel less chaotic when the difference and distance between two opposing forces is smaller. When you bring those differences together toward a calming center point, you will feel more at ease. Yin-yang helps explain the calm that arises from finding a center point amid chaotic extremes.

LEARNING TO CREATE ORDER IN EVERY ROOM OF THE HOME

The main principle of creating order is to design conditions that allow your mind to slow down. When a busy mind is trying to process lots of seemingly random stimuli, it has trouble calming itself. Your home must be a respite from the chaos of your day, from the moment you walk in the door until your head hits the pillow at night.

When people practice yoga or meditation, they set aside time to bring their minds into a calm, centered state. But if you can get your home to be an external version of that state, you can slip much more easily into a healthy frame of mind *simply by occupying your home and interacting with the space.* In the well-centered home, you bring the conditions of meditation into every moment.

So what does this look like in practical terms? To see how we can reduce some of the most common instances of chaos and overstimulation in the home, let's break it down by room.

Living Room

Many living rooms are bogged down with too many elements competing for attention. This is understandable, particularly if you have many treasures you want to display. But too much of a good thing can leave you subconsciously exhausted and overwhelmed.

Think of your living room as a piece of music. If every bar of the piece were played at full volume, the impact of a crescendo—the build-up of tension and excitement—would be lost. There are major aesthetic benefits to contrast.

To decide if your living room is overstimulating, sit down in your favorite chair and let your eyes wander. If you sense that your eyes are constantly moving from one thing to the next and have trouble finding a place to rest, your room lacks perceptible order. If this is the case, it's time to judiciously remove some of your belongings.

The first step, of course, is to remove clutter. Start by putting objects back where they belong. If you have things that don't have a home, you may need to invest in decorative boxes or drawer organizers to keep things neat and out of sight.

Clutter isn't limited to excess items that are out of place. It can also be a visual effect that results from having too many focal points in one room. If, after removing your extra items, you still find that your eyes can't rest in your living room, it's time for further correction. In a living room, there are typically three main things that compete to be the focal point: the television, the fireplace, and the view to the outdoors. If you have two or three of these in a room, you have to prioritize them according to your own taste. If you have a lovely view and value the calm that nature brings, arrange your furniture around that focal point and keep your television off to the side for more occasional use.

On the other hand, if the television is the key to your personal happiness and relaxation in the evenings, embrace that as your focal point. We all tend to discount the fact that we actually watch television—they're rarely featured in glossy home magazines—but we do. The television is a perfectly fine focal point if it supports your sense of calm and well-being.

In older homes, the fireplace is often given the place of honor in the living room. Frank Lloyd Wright, for instance, believed that the hearth was the center of family life, and he conveyed that message by the design and location of the fireplace in his homes—designs that remain hugely influential in the United States. But this was before television. In my work as an architect, I've taken to creating one element that has both a fireplace and a television in it. Neither is perfectly centered, but they balance each other within the element. It's also possible to mount a flat screen television above a low, linear fireplace to create a balance between two important focal points. I suggest avoiding placing a television above a traditional fireplace because that places the television too high on the wall and can cause neck problems.

There's no "right" answer when it comes to choosing your living room's focal point, as long as it makes you feel relaxed and at peace. Don't be afraid to test furniture arrangements around different focal points until you find the layout that works best for you. When it's right, you'll feel it.

 Quick Tip

Plato homebody types are more sensitive to chaos and need strong "editing" of spaces to keep visual stimuli from overwhelming. Experiment with removing focal points one by one until your eye no longer feels the need to jump from place to place—that's when Platos will feel truly at rest.

Kitchen

Kitchens contain so many working parts that it's important to follow the old adage: A place for everything, and everything in its place. Just like the living room, the first step is to take care of clutter. Organize small appliances and tools so they're handy but not overwhelming to the eye. Countertops don't need to be empty, but there should be sufficient workspace for food preparation in the spots where it makes the most sense. Tables and eating surfaces should also be kept clear of clutter. This is a prime example of the importance of maintenance, as kitchens can easily become chaotic if not attended to. Removing the pebbles that come in the form of crumbs, spills, and errant dishes is important for your overall sense of order.

When it comes to focal points, it helps to make one part of the kitchen the clear center of attention. This might be an island that stands out from the rest of the cabinetry with a different color or wood finish. It might be a decorative tile backsplash, or a range with a distinctive hood above it. Whatever you choose as the focal point, be sure to make it the star of the show and avoid having other elements compete for prominence. The kitchen is an easy place to have too many prima donnas vying for your attention—there's no need to put every magazine idea into one room.

I always advise my clients to pick their theme and then ruthlessly stick to it. Once you figure out your design objective, every other part of the kitchen can be included or rejected simply by looking at that new element and asking, *Does this support my objective or not?* If it doesn't fit in, or if it draws attention away from your primary focal point, let it go. You'll be happier in the end, even if it means letting an interesting tile choice or shiny appliance stay in the showroom.

Dining Room

When it comes to focal points, the dining room is one of the easiest rooms in the house, because the table and chairs always dominate the space. Even if they aren't placed in the center of the room, they're still the focus of the room's activity, so they naturally draw the eye to them. With table and chairs established, you need only make sure the other elements in the dining room are good supporting actors that work well with the style and character of the main eating area.

From a practical standpoint, you'll also want to keep items from piling up on the table and chairs, as clutter unrelated to your meal will ruin your sense of ease. A dining room has a singular purpose, so everything in the room should bolster your meal taking and interactions around the table.

If, like many people, you gravitate toward a more informal area of the home for eating, your formal dining room may become the place where you do your taxes and help the kids with homework. If that's the case on a daily basis, you don't really have a dining room anymore. And that's fine! But to center this space, you must deal with the room as you actually use it, not as its formal name suggests.

For example, if you find yourself using your so-called dining room as a home office, then treat it that way and provide places to store the paperwork, reference books, and supplies that are making their way into the space. This can be done by adding bookshelves or a credenza that you use not for serving dishes, but for neatly organized office supplies. This gives you the option to use the dining room for large gatherings a few times a year while allowing you to remove the sensory chaos that come from having too many functions in one space. When you make this mental leap to embrace how you *actually* use the space, you'll improve your quality of life on a daily basis.

When it comes to removing pebbles of chaos in the dining room, keeping the table clear is the most important thing you can do. This act is a gift to your future self: When you leave the room and reenter it later, you'll be met with a calming tableau that helps center you, rather than leave you agitated by clutter. Finding a place for your items and committing to keeping them there is the gift that keeps on giving.

Study or Office

The standard advice is to keep an orderly workspace by filing away papers and books that aren't in use. But let's be honest: This may not match your personal work method. If you have multiple projects or feel energized when surrounded by items that inspire you, a messy desk may actually support your working style. The key is to cultivate an awareness of your limit of disorder, and then hold the line. When you begin to feel agitated or have trouble concentrating, it's time to spend a half hour cleaning up your home office and filing items away in the storage units you've designated for them.

Everyone is different, so the best advice is to keep your personal antenna up to stay aware of your feelings in the space. If you find yourself allowing your workspace to tip over into chaos, make regular cleanup a priority. I learned to do this when the first architect I worked for established a Friday cleanup system. The whole team spent the last half-hour of the workweek cleaning up the drafting room so that we could walk into a fresh, clean office on Monday morning. It was a wonderful way to make sure we'd start each week with a fresh frame of mind. It also helped that the boss brought in some beers for everyone to enjoy while we worked!

This type of routine also works for your home at large. Consider gathering the family or your roommates for a quick cleanup at the same time each week, and offer a reward to enjoy together when you're done. Whether you have Friday pizza pick-ups or Sunday afternoon sandwiches and cleaning, working together on a routine basis becomes fun, and the rewards of togetherness are doubled when you get to enjoy your chaos-free space for another week.

Bedroom

Like keeping the dining table clear, the simple act of making the bed can make a serious difference in your state of mind when you return to rest each night. A rumpled pile of blankets and sheets triggers disorder in your mind and makes it more difficult to settle into a restful mode. This isn't about impressing someone. It's about enhancing the restorative benefit of sleep at night, so it's truly worth the five minutes of effort.

If you have limited space that requires you to use your bedroom for other activities, it's important to use some screening techniques to create a barrier between the areas, so you don't find yourself staring at exercise equipment or a desk full of work as you try to drift off. You can use a folding screen, a large potted plant, or a judiciously placed bookcase to define that space so it's mentally no longer part of your bedroom. If you're really pressed for space, lighting can help define areas as well—keep your workspace well-lit during the day but in the dark and out of mind when you're heading for bed.

Bathroom

Like the kitchen, bathrooms are functional rooms that should be orderly, though it's not necessary to have every surface completely clear at all times. For most people, it makes sense to have items like toothbrushes, soap, and the like within easy reach. Less-used items can be stowed in the medicine cabinet or in the vanity to reduce visual clutter.

Beyond these basics, it's important to note that mirrors and an abundance of shiny surfaces in bathrooms can present too much stimulation. At all costs, avoid having mirrors opposite each other so you don't get an endlessly reflected tunneling effect. I also recommend installing a dimmer switch in the bathroom to reduce glare—a particularly welcome addition when nature calls in the middle of the night.

Bathrooms also create sensory chaos in the form of sounds, which tend to echo off of all those hard surfaces. Adding plush towels and bath mats will help dampen reflected sound, so consider adding a towel bar or two as space allows to create a quiet sanctuary.

Patio or Porch

Patios and porches are ideal for letting your earth-grounding choices calm your mind and helping your brain sort through the excess stimulation of the day. To make these areas more useful throughout the year, add a ceiling fan for summer and a radiant heater for spring and fall. In this way, you can extend the usefulness of these areas and take advantage of the calming effects of nature as often as possible. By setting up an inviting place of retreat, you'll have an emotional recharging station where you can let the chaos of the day melt away from you as you become more centered and calm.

The Ancient Art of Centering in a Modern World

Centering is an ancient concept that involves visualization to focus on the present and takes power away from the distractions of the outside world. As your focus moves inward, negative thoughts are subdued. Training in the technique of centering helps you control your body's reactions to external stimuli and restores your essential positive energy, often referred to as *chi* or *ki*. When your mind redirects this vital energy to the center of the body, your mind clears and you gain a sense of inner calm.

This technique has gained popularity among athletes to improve their performances, but anyone can enjoy the benefits of centering. Because we are so strongly influenced by the "built environment" that we interact with during most of our lives, our homes exert a strong influence on our degree of centeredness. By making your home a well-centered home, you increase its positive centering effect on you, which allows you to enjoy the benefits of centering simply by living your life in a beautiful, calming place.

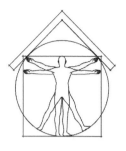

Chapter 8

HOW FORMS AND MATERIALS TRANSFORM YOUR HOME—AND YOUR MOOD!

Architecture is the art and science of enclosing and defining spaces, and one of its basic tools is the manipulation of form. Form is what happens when we begin to mark off space in the home, whether with walls, ceilings, or other design elements. But no forms can be created without specific building blocks, or materials. Forms and materials work hand in hand to create the particular qualities you wish to experience in your home.

FORMS AND THEIR EFFECT ON THE PSYCHE

First, let's begin by defining what we mean by *form*. A form is a two- or three-dimensional object. A form is usually more than a singular basic shape, though it definitely includes all the geometric shapes you learned in school. As an architectural concept, form is the total assembly and organization of those shapes to create a coherent impression. Forms can be solids or voids. They can be the objects in the room or they can be the spaces that the floor, walls, and ceiling of a room define.

For example, consider the form that influences us the most, the human form. It's a complex shape that we easily recognize as distinct from trees and from other animals. It's made up of many recognizable parts that can be broken down easily into geometric shapes: circles for eyes, semicircles for ears, and so on. Likewise, your house is made up of many simple shapes and parts that combine to create an overall impression you immediately recognize as the form you call *home*. The trick in dealing with forms is to skillfully arrange and manipulate them so that the impression is one of harmony and balance.

Forms carry meanings that we respond to innately, such as the way a baby is drawn toward the human face, and meanings based on cultural and personal experiences. Consider the differences in art and architecture in different cultures, for example. Certain forms elicit a predictable emotional response, which makes it easier to harness their power in architecture. In 2010, neuroscientists at Johns Hopkins University designed a study to see what shapes were most pleasing.[7] Specifically, they wanted to find out what happens in the human brain when we look at certain forms.

To do this, researchers chose twenty-five shapes and their variations from an abstract sculpture that did not resemble any familiar object and asked subjects to rate them in order of preference. They also took MRI scans to track brain activity as subjects looked at the images. The researchers found that people preferred images with gentle curves over those with sharp points. In addition, the curved shapes produced increased brain activity. Researchers speculated that curved forms relate to the organic natural world and suggest good health, whereas angular objects relate to inanimate, inorganic objects. It would seem that we respond strongly to nature—further evidence of the importance of earth-grounding!

These results also translate specifically to architecture. Another study published in the *Proceedings of the National Academy of Sciences* showed participants two hundred images of furnished rooms.[8] Some had round columns

---

[7] Gambino, Megan. "Do Our Brains Find Certain Shapes More Attractive Than Others?" *Scientific American.* 14 Nov. 2013. Accessed 9 Mar. 2020. https://www.smithsonianmag.com/science-nature/do-our-brains-find-certain-shapes-more-attractive-than-others-180947692/

[8] Vartania, Oshan, et al. "Impact of contour on aesthetic judgments and approach-avoidance decisions in architecture." *Proceedings of the*

and furniture with curved edges, while others had boxy couches and tables with crisp edges. Brain scans taken while volunteers were viewing the images showed that the rounded décor initiated more brain activity, just as the Johns Hopkins study found.

How Forms Define the Home

Your relationship to the form of a home begins with its exterior. The physical manifestation of your home should look and feel like home. In most cultures, a basic box with a triangular or pyramidal shape above it conveys the meaning of shelter. Though born out of the practical need to provide cover from the rain and snow on the rooftop, the slanted roof form has become a strong symbol for safety and security.

Architecture that tries to deny our long-standing cultural connection to these forms usually fails. There are too many centuries of human experience cementing certain impressions in our minds. For the majority of people, metal boxes with flat roofs and no overhangs do not connect with the concept of home, so it's a major task to get them to see ultra-modern residential architecture as shelter instead of a shipping container. That's simply not a place to live, even though it may be appealing in a sculptural way.

National Academy of Sciences in the United States of America. 18 Jun. 2013. Accessed 9 Mar. 2020. https://www.pnas.org/content/110/Supplement_2/10446.short

The architecture of Frank Lloyd Wright provides wonderful examples of working with forms in a way that evokes a sense of shelter both inside and out. Though his ideas were revolutionary at the time, Wright never strayed far from our collective idea of what a home should look like. He favored long, low forms and accentuated horizontal lines to relate to the flat sweeps of prairie in the American Midwest. The forms are restful and relaxing, while his deep roof overhangs projected a strong sense of security.

Wright punctuated those horizontal forms with a major vertical element: the hearth. Vertical forms command attention and help the mind create hierarchies of importance based on height. Wright's fireplaces were the warmest, most secure portions of his homes, so they became natural places to gather—and people were given a visual cue to do so by the height and material of the hearth.

Though most homes are designed with strong lines and sharp angles that make up square and rectangular spaces, comforting curves need to be introduced throughout to create a sense of coziness and connect to the natural world. This is often done with furnishings as well as elements such as rounded trim moulding, handrails, arches, and windows.

Shelter as a Cultural Shape

A child's basic drawing of a house is likely to consist of a square with a triangle on top. That's all it takes to drum up an image of home in the mind's eye. It's one of the most powerful symbols human beings have, and it's the sloped, sheltering roof that has taken on particular resonance as a form.

This important form is seen across cultures and languages. For example, the Chinese ideogram that signifies "house" starts with two sloping lines atop a base, very much like a child's drawing of a house. From there, the same roof form is transformed into ideograms for "family," "peace," and "resting place" by adding other forms to that basic house shape, thus showing the strong cultural connections among these concepts.

Likewise, the sign for "house" in American Sign Language begins with that same peaked roof extending over solid walls. We are so attuned to rooflines, in fact, that I have had architectural clients specifically request bedrooms that feature ceiling areas where the slanted roof clips into the corners of the room. These forms send the powerful message of security, so they're ideal for creating cozy bedrooms.

ASSESSING THE FORMS IN YOUR HOME

If you're curious about how all the forms in your home work together to create a sense of shelter and calm, it's a good idea to take inventory of them. Start with your favorite room and take photos of it from several angles. Print the photos out—no need to get fancy with special paper, or even to print them in color, since you're going to use the pictures as worksheets.

Place the photos on a table and rotate them so they are upside down. This simple shift will help you begin to see the forms in your space without associating them with actual objects. Grab a pencil or pen and begin outlining the shapes you see, and then highlight the ones you feel most drawn to.

If you're having trouble with this exercise, think about the game I Spy, in which you often describe something in the room by naming its shape or color. Children are very good at picking out geometric shapes in unexpected places, so embrace your inner child—or even get a real child to help you!—as you search for forms and shapes to outline.

When considering forms in your home, it's important to remember that voids—the spaces between walls and other elements—are also forms. The shapes you see could well be made of thin air, existing only because they are outlined by walls and furniture. For example, a standing mirror might create a tall triangle between it and the wall that becomes a very obvious form in the room. Keep your eyes and mind open to the possibilities, and soon you'll see forms interacting with each other everywhere you look.

Repeat this exercise for your least favorite room as well, and then compare the forms you noticed. Are there forms that are more common in your favorite space than in your least favorite space? This can help you determine which forms really speak to you and give you some welcome inspiration to add them as pearls to other areas of your home.

A Glossary of Forms for the Home

Before you dive into assessing the various forms throughout your home, it will help to know exactly what you're looking for. What follows is a list of the most common forms in residential architecture and interior decor, along with the feelings and ideas they tend to evoke. Use this list to help you identify existing forms and choose the forms of new elements you'd like to add as part of the centering process. For instance, if you are in the market for a new couch, you can narrow your choices down to designs with forms that create the atmosphere you want to achieve in your living room.

Just as you couldn't possibly use every word in the dictionary to write a poem, you're also not meant to incorporate every one of these forms into your home. In fact, if you overwhelm the space with too many different forms, they'll lose their power and end up creating cacophony instead of a restful theme.

- **Squares and Cubes:** These basic building blocks are perfectly balanced and suggest regularity and order. They're an economical, efficient way to break up space, and they create a sense of dependability and security.

- **Triangles and Pyramids:** Like the peaked roofs that symbolize shelter, these shapes evoke a strong sense of permanence. Triangles can bear tremendous weight without breaking, so these shapes feel powerful and stable.

- **Circles and Spheres:** Balanced, round forms suggest infinity, as they have no obvious starting or ending point. They may also inspire thoughts of the earth, sun, and planets. These forms relate well to the human hand and call out to be touched. They also reflect light smoothly, with a gradual transition from the lighted side to the shadowed side instead of creating harsh shadows with precise edges.

- **Horizontal Slabs:** Rectangular forms that run horizontally connect to the ground and greatly enhance earth-grounding. Floorboards and tiles or bricks in a running bond pattern are subtle examples of these forms.

- **Arches:** Arches are an example of a form that relies as much on void as its actual material. Arches suggest division between two areas as well as a feeling of welcoming, of being invited to pass through them. Because arches welcome people to enter a space, they help suggest the human presence as discussed in Chapter 5. Arches also exude strength, as they prop up walls and keep everything held in place.

- **Straight Lines:** Straight lines draw the eye in a particular direction and imply movement. As straight lines form sharp edges and angles, they inject energy and a feeling of purpose into a space.

- **Curved Lines:** Curved lines imply flowing motion and tend to slow the eye as it wanders over the form. Curved lines are soothing, comforting, and tend to be the preferred shape among humans, likely due to their organic nature. These are particularly appealing to Nightingale homebody types.

- **Spirals:** Spirals invite contemplation as they draw the eye around and around again—an experience akin to walking the spiraling paths of a meditation labyrinth. Like circles, they suggest infinity, but they are also mathematically quite precise. Natural spirals like a conch shell follow the Fibonacci sequence, a ratio that has been deemed pleasing to the eye by philosophers and artists throughout history. Astaire homebody types especially enjoy the flowing motion of spirals.

- **Organic Forms:** These forms originate in nature rather than geometry; however, a lot of geometry can be found in nature. Organic forms can be shaped like leaves, flowers, animals, and other natural forms that are easily identified. These are also excellent for adding a sense of ease and enhancing earth-grounding.

- **Fractal Forms:** These forms have a shape that is divided into smaller versions of that shape in increments, particularly towards the edges. For example, trees that begin with a large trunk and gradually diminish down to branches and then twigs are fractal forms. Likewise, a set of Russian nesting dolls that repeats the form while getting progressively smaller is a fractal form. These thought-provoking forms are especially beloved by Plato and Galileo homebody types.

- **Free Forms:** Draped cloth, windblown snowdrifts, and sand at the bottom of an hourglass are examples of free forms. These are abstractions that can provide an interesting counterbalance to geometrics. They're best used in small doses as an accent, as they're often too ephemeral or hard to control to serve as primary forms in the home.

USEFUL TIPS FOR WORKING WITH FORMS IN YOUR HOME

No matter what your budget, you can find ways to make the most of the forms in your home. By making wise choices, you can use them to better channel the energy of your home to create a more restful environment.

($) Getting Started with Limited Funds

- **Add round forms to center your home.** Round forms are scientifically proven to be pleasing to the eye. One easy way to incorporate these forms into your living spaces is to choose a round or oval area rug. Use it under the dining table or as the anchor to a conversational seating arrangement to foster interaction.

- **Use forms as spatial definers.** Like the lone tree in a meadow, a hanging light fixture commands the space around it. Place a hanging fixture a few steps in from the front door to define the entry and enhance its importance as an in-between space bridging the outside and the inside.

($) ($) Investing in the Future

- **Create consistency with furniture.** If a room is predominantly furnished with rounded, organic shapes, it makes sense to keep that look consistent throughout. Sharp, angular forms might be intrusions to the flow and should be replaced with pieces with rounded corners and edges that work with the overall feel of the room.

- **Add decorative pendant lights.** Pendants with rounded forms can help soften kitchen workspaces. When the fixtures relate to the scale of the hand, they also work as inviting elements that people the space. Place them above the seating area at a kitchen counter or island to signal its purpose and welcome people to relax.

$ $ $ Making Major Changes

- **Use forms to control the visual height of a room.** Add decorative ceiling beams to break down and humanize the scale of high ceilings. Beams can draw the eye in a way that makes the room feel wider, but they should always run across the room the "short" way, as this is the way actual structural beams would run.

- **Add rounded crown moulding.** Moulding with a concave "cove" shape can give a room more grace than traditional Colonial-style mouldings. Cove crown mouldings do a better job of containing the energy in a room and are a prime example of how a single change can have an outsized impact on the way your home feels.

- **Replace oddly shaped windows.** A single arch-topped transom in a room with predominately rectangular windows and forms can appear out of place and disrupt the flow. Though these were popular in recent decades, removing or replacing these anomalies will bring your home up to date and remove an all-too-common design pebble.

THE LANGUAGE OF MATERIALS IN THE HOME

Materials are much easier to define than forms: they are simply what things are made of. But the materials have a language of their own; they speak to us based on our senses, not just our knowledge of how they perform in given conditions. They vary in how they interact with light, how they feel in hand, how they appear they *might* feel, their hardness or softness, and the sounds they make when we interact with them. All of these qualities combine to elicit different emotions, so deepening your understanding of materials and their meanings will help you choose the right ones for your home.

Materials can be divided into two categories: man-made materials, such as glass, metal, and plastics, which aren't found in nature and must be manufactured; and natural materials, such as wood, cotton, and stone, which come directly from nature. Natural materials can be further divided into those that are in their natural state and those that people have altered substantially. Rough-hewn beams in an old home are close to the natural state of the wood, while a highly carved and polished oak bureau shows more work of the human hand.

Just as shapes, textures, and colors are arranged to form the composition of a painting, materials in your home deserve similar consideration as you create the composition of a room. Unlike a painting, however, many materials in your home must also serve a functional purpose. For example, your kitchen backsplash should be water resistant, so a wallpaper made of woven sisal would be a poor choice in this location, no matter how beautiful it may be. This tension between form and function is the key factor that separates architecture from sculpture. In the end, your home must be a place to live in, not just to look at.

As you assess the materials in your home, you are above all striving for comfortable compositions. To do this, choose materials that enhance the peopling effect discussed in Chapter 5: carved wood, clay pots, and other items that show how people have cared for and manipulated the materials to create something beautiful. You'll also want to choose materials that express comfort and security on their own.

Remember, creating a sense of security does not mean physical safety so much as emotional safety. Upholstery that makes noise when you move, for instance, destroys the sense of emotional security by startling or irritating you.

Because we interact so closely with materials, it's important to remain vigilant for anything that could become a pebble in your daily life and substitute it for a more appropriate option—especially if that other option can go beyond neutral to become a pearl by enhancing the centering of your home.

A GLOSSARY OF MATERIALS FOR THE HOME

Materials influence our senses of sight, touch, and hearing. We respond to how they look, how they feel, and even how they affect the acoustics in the room. What follows is a list of some of the most common materials found in homes and how they may affect your mood. Knowing their effect will help you choose wisely to create a calming or energizing space as appropriate.

- **Wood:** Wood is an earth-grounding material because of its natural source, and it is a peopling material because it expresses the efforts of another person to cut and shape it. Wood also looks and feels warm to the touch, which adds comfort to the home. Wood on walls and ceilings further increases the feeling of warmth and comfort—as long as it does not make the room dark and dreary. Wood-paneled rooms need ample windows for natural light and good artificial lighting to avoid gloominess.

- **Stone and Tile:** Stone and tile are also strong earth-grounding materials that express strength and durability. Unlike wood, they look and feel hard and cold, so they should be used sparingly in living spaces and sleeping spaces. Stone or tile floors will make a room acoustically lively, meaning that sounds will echo more. This quality gives the room a cold feeling without actually touching the material. Because stone is not absorbent, it is a good material in entryways, bathrooms, and kitchens. Polished stone, due to its reflective qualities, is perceived as being colder and harder than non-polished stone, but carved or chiseled stone can provide a peopling effect as you subconsciously connect with the person who shaped the stone in the past.

- **Metal:** Metals are perceived as the coldest of all materials and should be used only as judicious accent pieces. In rooms like the kitchen that must have a lot of metal, use softer, warmer materials to offset the hard, uninviting message the metal sends to the subconscious. Natural or painted wood cabinets, or even stone countertops with honed or "leathered" finishes, are good choices for creating a more welcoming room.

- **Fabric:** Fabrics are highly tactile and send clear messages about how they would feel simply due to their appearance. Rough, woven materials are generally less tactilely inviting than finer weaves, though this perception also depends on whether the material appears plush and fluffy like chenille yarn or scratchy like sisal. Shiny, satiny surfaces look soothing and cool. They call out to be touched, so it's no surprise that blankets often have a satin edge to tuck under your chin and that young children's fingers always go to the smooth, satin parts of their stuffed animals.

$ Quick Tip

The easiest way to introduce fabrics into a room is with throw pillows. Choose satin for a cool, inviting feel, rich velvet to indicate warmth, or textured weaves to add interest to any seating area. And don't be afraid to include some faux fur just for the fun of it. It can be mesmerizing to let your fingers rub across fur.

HOW MATERIALS RESONATE WITH DIFFERENT HOMEBODY TYPES

Material selection is a highly personalized endeavor, and you'll likely find that you gravitate toward certain textures and appearances more than others. The trick is to balance the overall composition of materials so that your room is neither too cold and edgy nor overcrowded with competing elements.

If you're not quite sure what materials speak to you, I encourage you to consider your homebody type as discovered in the quiz in Chapter 2. Each personality type has materials that resonate and support it, so this is a useful starting point for discovering how to accent your home with materials that will make you feel more centered.

Materials for Astaire Homebody Types

Astaire homebody types love to command a group's attention and therefore feel at ease with harder surfaces that reflect sound. Consider a healthy dose of modern design materials such as glossy ceramic or glass tiles, metal panels, and glass tabletops. Polished surfaces and accents that glitter and shine create energy in spaces reserved for entertaining and are ideal for creating the bold statements that Astaire types love.

Materials for Galileo Homebody Types

Galileo homebody types have a deep appreciation for materials that express the wonder of nature: stone with an amalgam of minerals, wood with exotic color or graining, and fibers in their near-natural form. Alabaster or onyx make particularly nice accents due to their translucence, which adds a layer of interest. Galileo types are also drawn to tile, fabrics, or wall coverings with geometric patterns and tessellations that hint at the mathematical order of things.

Materials for Nightingale Homebody Types

As nurturers, Nightingale homebody types respond strongly to soft materials and rounded upholstered forms. Voluminous fabric draperies are ideal, though care should be taken not to interfere with the benefits of sunlight. Nightingales prefer materials that invite people to gather, so furniture must not look cold or stiff. An abundance of throw pillows and blankets in soft fabrics will add a sense of warmth to plush, inviting furniture.

 ## Materials for Plato Homebody Types

Plato homebody types are philosophical by nature and are fascinated by materials that have a story behind them. Hand-woven fabrics, hand-hewn wood, chiseled stone, and hand-painted tiles are all fine examples of materials that inspire wonder for Plato types. Likewise, historical materials like wood flooring with visible nails or reclaimed materials that had a previous life will inspire contemplation, the highest form of centering for Plato types.

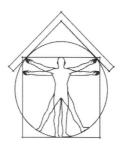

Chapter 9

VISUAL RHYTHMS AND PATTERNS THAT CALM THE MIND

Architecture and interior design are built not only around the forms discussed in Chapter 8, but also around the patterns and visual rhythms those forms combine to create. Understanding how these elements come together will allow you to choose patterns that work together harmoniously to settle the mind and create a flow of energy in your home that feels "just right."

THE DIFFERENCE BETWEEN PATTERNS AND VISUAL RHYTHMS

We're all familiar with patterns in the general sense of the word. Patterns are everywhere: tartan plaids, wallpaper designs, and repeating images on fabrics are common examples. A pattern is essentially any planned, purposeful arrangement of parts that features repeating elements. It does not matter whether the "planner" of the pattern was a human being, a higher power, or Mother Nature. What matters is that the pattern can be perceived.

To understand how the eye interacts with a pattern, imagine an accent wall covered in patterned wallpaper. Your eye can move in any direction across the wall—up, down, left, or right—and you will still experience the repetition. Patterns draw your eye across a repeating grid and are therefore fairly energetic in that they create a sense of movement in your field of vision.

When we think of patterns as grids, it becomes clear that there are many more patterns around us than just decorative fabrics or wallpaper. Floor and backsplash tiles, cedar shingle siding, brick patios, and even the grid created by the divided lights of windows all offer subtle patterning that is repeated across a large area.

Visual rhythms, on the other hand, are more linear and tend to draw the eye across them in one direction. Rhythms are a sequential arrangement of elements, such as colonnades, arcades, rows of windows, and stepping-stones that draw the eye along a single line. Rhythms are less mathematically rigid than patterns and can feel more organic, as when a gardener creates a rhythm by planting daisies at intervals along a flower border. The plants aren't perfectly spaced, but the repetition of similar flowers draws the eye through the garden in a pleasing rhythm.

Visual rhythms come in four varieties:

- **Regular Rhythms:** These are rhythms in which elements are arranged at equal intervals, like the beating of a healthy heart. Tiles of equal size and shape, floorboards of equal width, and a flight of stairs are all examples of regular rhythms.

- **Alternating Rhythms:** These rhythms place elements with unequal spacing but with a repeating pattern, such as wide-narrow-wide-narrow. These are a bit more interesting than regular rhythms and keep the brain more occupied, so they inject more energy into a room than regular rhythms.

- **Random Rhythms:** These rhythms are made up of repeating elements that occur at no set interval. The elements are scattered at random, but they imply a pattern. Examples are stars or clouds across the sky or the rocks in a fieldstone wall. These rhythms are highly engaging because they challenge the mind to find or create repetition out of chaos.

- **Progressive Rhythms:** These rhythms are created with similar elements of varying sizes. Examples are concentric circles or a series of concentric arches that appear to shrink as they stretch toward the vanishing point on the horizon. Window and door mouldings with interesting profiles tend to feature progressive rhythms, as do pathways that gradually widen as they reach their destination.

In contrast to patterns, visual rhythms tend to provide a sense of calm, because there's less stimulation for the brain to sort through—there's only one way for the eye to be guided, so you are visually led to an endpoint instead of choosing where to look across a pattern. An allée of trees or shrubs along the driveway, shiplap boards on walls or ceilings, and long wooden floorboards are all examples of common visual rhythms found in the home.

There's a good deal of overlap between patterns and visual rhythms, of course, and differentiating between them isn't really the point. The main thing to be aware of is just how many patterns and visual rhythms surround you, so you can harness their effect to enhance your mood throughout your home. Once you understand how patterns and visual rhythms work on your mind, you can make choices that enhance your centering and well-being.

A Note on Textures

There is a point at which a pattern gets to be too small to be perceived as a grid or series of distinct elements. When this happens, we perceive the item as a whole entity with a particular texture rather than a pattern.

continued on the next page...

A Note on Textures

...continued

To understand the difference, imagine two different tile floors. The first has large 12" x 12" tiles forming a checkerboard. In this case, it's easy to pick out the pattern beneath your feet. The second floor, however, has little 1" x 1" tiles, as you may find in a bathroom. In this case, it's harder to detect the pattern and you experience the floor as a whole—especially if it's only one color. In this case, you have a floor with texture rather than pattern.

Most textures have a pattern, but some are nearly microscopic. You don't often notice the individual fibers that make up a woven textile, but you feel the textured weave, and you experience it with your eyes as whole cloth.

THE POWER OF PATTERNS AND VISUAL RHYTHMS

Rhythm is the drumbeat in music. It sets the cadence and timing of a song with tight, frequently repeated sounds. Fast, energetic rhythms have many beats in a short space, while slower, more soothing songs have the beats spread out from each other.

Just as the rhythmic beat provides an organizing force to music, visual rhythms do the same thing in our homes.

Visual rhythms and patterns set the perceived pace of the space by adding energy or promoting calm. They provide a structure for organizing the otherwise chaotic visual stimuli we encounter each day. Remember, our minds seek order out of chaos, so we need a mental structure to provide order. When we perceive a more orderly world, our minds become more peaceful.

It's useful to remember that our bodies also have rhythms of their own. The heart beats at a regular pace that reverberates through the body and serves as a timekeeper. Our digestive system, sleep cycle, and even our mental alertness all respond to the rhythms of the earth, sun, and moon. We are happiest and most mindful when our biological rhythms operate in harmony with the cycles of the world around us. The visual patterns we sense through our eyes influence our internal rhythms, so a well-centered home supports overall well-being by providing calming patterns.

We intuitively sense that some patterns are more energetic than others. Those with many lines, shapes, or elements in a small area force the eye to move rapidly across them, in much the same way the fast beat of a song drives you to dance. In patterns where the elements are more spread out—and particularly ones that have more curving or wave-like elements—the eye moves more slowly and smoothly. It doesn't have to jump from one thing to the other.

We have a word for this in English: *busy*. When we say a pattern is busy, it's because we feel the sensation of movement and energy it brings to our eyes and our brains. Busy patterns can work well in public areas where you wish to entertain, but they should be avoided in places where you want to rest or meditate.

It's also important to remember that patterns and visual rhythms are entertainment for the eye and the mind. A series of blank walls, floors, and ceilings and groups of objects that are untextured and uniformly colored are the visual equivalent of music with no variations to the timing and only notes in a narrow range. It's too boring to be effective! Likewise, homes with limited rhythms and patterns are pebbles that need to be dealt with. Police interrogation rooms and solitary confinement cells are devoid of visual interest for a reason: they reduce a suspect's mental defenses—something you certainly don't want your home to do to you.

Quick Tip

Always the entertainer, Astaire homebody types are also highly attuned to auditory rhythm. To appeal to a highly developed sense of musicality, consider keeping staircases uncarpeted to allow rhythmic footsteps to be heard throughout the home.

HOW TO USE VISUAL RHYTHMS AND PATTERNS IN THE WELL-CENTERED HOME

When working with patterns, it's important to be thoughtful about what you add to the space. Patterns, textures, and visual rhythms are a must-have in any space to add interest, but you should always take the time to assess how a particular pattern makes you feel. Is it tight and energetic—*busy*—or more languid and fluid? Becoming attuned to the cadence of a pattern will help you choose the ones that support what you're trying to achieve in a particular room. These "just right" patterns then become pearls in your decor.

To design spaces that are calming and centering, look for patterns that feel complete rather than ambiguous. Patterns that allow your eyes to move across them slowly, at the rate of your heartbeat, are ideal. This isn't an exact science, but as you sit and look at different patterns, you'll build your capacity for feeling them accurately. If it feels restful to you and encourages you to take in a deep breath, you'll know you've found one that works.

Visual rhythms that repeat at a human scale are also ideal for the well-centered home. They might relate to the size of the hand, like the width of shiplap paneling or wooden floorboards, or they might relate to the size of a footstep, like large pavers or stepping-stones. Rows of columns, arches, or large windows should relate to the size of the human body as a whole to best people the space as discussed in Chapter 5.

A final word of advice: don't create visual rhythms or choose patterns that are all the same scale. In an orchestra or a band, the musicians aren't all playing the same thing. They play to the same tempo, but each part is actually made of up different patterns of notes and rhythms. These individual patterns work together to make something different and better than the individual parts. It's the *gestalt*, or the organized whole that is greater than the sum of its parts. This is what you achieve when you carefully select patterns that work together to create the energy you want in your home.

PATTERNS FOR EVERY PERSONALITY

Now that you have a sense of how patterns and visual rhythms stimulate the mind in different ways, you probably won't be surprised to learn that certain patterns resonate with people according to their personalities. Just as each homebody type tends toward certain shapes, so too do they gravitate toward particular patterns and visual rhythms.

If you're uncertain how to begin your work with patterns, refer back to Chapter 8 to see what shapes work best with your homebody type, and use those as a starting point as you consider adding patterns in the form of fabrics or wallpaper—that is, you can begin your search by looking for patterns that contain your preferred shapes.

Next, consider how the overall feel of patterns and visual rhythms will influence your mood. Add busier, energetic patterns to areas where you want to feel alert and more restful rhythms to your bedroom and areas where you wish to feel calm. As a guide, I've included specific advice for each of the homebody types as a jumping-off point for your journey into working with visual rhythms.

Visual Rhythms for Astaire Homebody Types

Astaire homebody types prefer strong, obvious patterns and visual rhythms with regular intervals, but don't be afraid to punctuate patterns with an occasional change to add interest. For example, a highly regular pattern of square or rectangular tiles on a kitchen backsplash could be even more appealing with a few contrasting colors scattered across the pattern for punctuation.

Astaire types will also appreciate patterns within patterns as a way to add energy and interest to decor. For example, a staircase with three balusters connecting the railing to each step would benefit from the addition of extra patterning of the center baluster. This baluster could sport carvings for interest or have portions painted to accent its profile. With every center baluster made to stand out, you've created a pattern within a pattern that provides a shot of energy to the whole staircase.

Visual Rhythms for Galileo Homebody Types

Mathematically minded Galileo homebody types appreciate geometric patterns above all others. They also enjoy patterns that are further divided into sub-patterns. For example, paneled walls that are subdivided with insets or made with alternating widths of board will keep Galileo types intellectually engaged.

When it comes to visual rhythms, Galileo types respond to rhythms created with three-dimensional objects rather than just lines. Instead of relying on divided lights in windows and the horizontal lines of shiplap, try arranging decorative storage boxes, pottery, and other pieces of artwork in such a way that you create a rhythm with their forms, whether on a single shelf or across a whole room.

Visual Rhythms for Nightingale Homebody Types

As nurturers, Nightingale homebody types respond to organic, flowing rhythms that resonate peace: think ocean waves, curling vines, and fluttering leaves. These natural rhythms may appear random, but it's the organic repetition that appeals to Nightingale types rather than a rigid geometric or linear pattern.

Remember too that Nightingales, more than any other homebody type, enjoy the curved lines that humans are naturally drawn to. That means visual rhythms arranged in curves or circles are most appealing. For example, instead of placing decorative objects in a line along a mantel or dining table, place objects in an arc or sweeping S-curve. These gentle rhythms are soothing and help Nightingale types feel at peace.

Visual Rhythms for Plato Homebody Types

Contemplative Plato homebody types revel in subtle patterns that may not be obvious at first glance. For example, try a tile floor with two or three colors that are only slightly different, laid in a pattern that takes a bit of observation to discern. Platos enjoy becoming absorbed in subtleties and will revel in the *aha!* moment they feel when the brain untangles the "rules" of a complex pattern.

When creating visual rhythms, rely on the scale of the human body when placing objects. For example, the hand and fingers are useful tools for spacing items on your desktop or bookshelf to create a pleasing rhythm with neither too much nor too little space between objects.

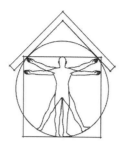

Chapter 10

TUNING IN TO THE SENSES: PRACTICAL ADVICE FOR THE EYES, EARS, AND MORE

Our senses are our tools for interacting with the world. Sights and sounds give our brains a good deal of information to process, and our reactions to the ones in our home will be positive or negative—pearls we enjoy or pebbles in our shoe that irritate us and prevent us from feeling centered.

Many of the adverse stimuli that affect our senses fly below our radar, irritating us in a subliminal way that can be hard to define. To raise your awareness, try performing a full sensory room scan. Sit in the center of the room and slowly look over every inch to take in all the visual stimuli, noting what brings pleasure and what is an annoyance.

Then, close your eyes and allow the ambient sounds of the room to wash over you. Allow several minutes to elapse so you can tune in to the quieter sounds that you may not ordinarily notice. In this way, you can begin to sharpen your senses and work with the existing stimuli in your home.

EASY ON THE EYES: THE IMPORTANCE OF PROPER HOME LIGHTING

Everyone's room scan will reveal different pebbles and pearls, but I'd like to draw your attention to an element that too often goes ignored yet affects every visual stimulus in your home: the lighting.

Lighting can be a pebble or a pearl. It can be annoyingly inadequate, or it can set the perfect mood and calibrate our internal clocks. Yet most people don't spend much time thinking about the lighting in their homes. To focus your attention, consider these common pebbles and pearls and how you may address them to keep your visual stimuli pleasurable and centering.

Common Lighting Pebbles to Address

- **Lack of Natural Light:** The sun is the only full-spectrum light source we have, so natural light makes colors more vivid. Because everything looks better in natural light, you want as much of it as possible. Open curtains and blinds during the day to let the sun shine in. Keep north-facing windows uncovered all the time, as this gentle, even light is the most consistent throughout the day.

- **Unwanted Shadows:** A poorly placed artificial light can cast shadows that make it hard to work or simply make things look bad. This is common in kitchens with a single overhead light, but you can add under-cabinet lighting to shine directly onto countertops to fill in the shadows. Overhead lighting in bathrooms is another culprit, as harsh downlighting casts shadows on your face that make you look older and tired. Adding wall sconces on either side of your mirror will even out these shadows and make you feel much better about yourself early in the morning.

- **Fluorescent Flickering:** Fluorescent lights—both the tube type and the curly type—flicker at a rate that's below our visual perception but can still trigger migraines, agitation, or fatigue.[9] These are the kinds of stress reactions you want to avoid in your well-centered home. Energy-efficient LEDs are a much better choice because they don't flicker

---

[9] Dunckley, Victoria L. "Why CFLs Aren't Such a Bright Idea." *Psychology Today*. Sep. 15, 2014. Accessed Mar. 26, 2020. https://www.psychologytoday.com/us/blog/mental-wealth/201409/why-cfls-arent-such-bright-idea

and aren't filled with toxic mercury that requires special disposal.

- **Improper Color Temperature:** LED lights are long-lasting and require very little electricity, but choose wisely. Many emit a great deal of blue light, which makes your rooms feel cold and harsh and can disrupt your body's internal clock.[10] Before you buy, check the bulb's color temperature, which should be between 2,700K and 3,000K on the Kelvin scale to ensure a warm, pleasant wash of light similar to incandescent bulbs. Avoid those harsh, bluish white lights (5,000K) that were typical of the first generation of LED lights. For the best results, look for bulbs that also have a Color Rendering Index (CRI) score of 80 or above, which will ensure that the colors in your room look vibrant rather than gray. All good LED lights will have this information printed on the packaging.

$ Quick Tip

All those little blue and green lights on chargers and electronics seem dim in the daytime but can be bright enough to disrupt your sleep at night. Keep them out of the bedroom or cover them with a piece of electrical tape to solve this problem for pennies, and you will sleep better.

---

[10] Ibid.

Lighting Pearls to Enhance Your Enjoyment

- **Dimmer Switches:** Dimmers are very useful in controlling the intensity of light. They also give you much more control over the mood of the space. Dimmers are a great way to get several types of lighting out of one fixture, and they're inexpensive and easy to install—you can even do it yourself with a few simple tools. Just be sure to cut the power at the breaker before attempting any electrical work.

- **Layered Lighting:** Instead of relying on a single overhead fixture, each room should have several light sources, including "wall washers" around the perimeter, accent lighting to highlight artwork, and individual lamps. A complete lighting plan for a hallway, for example, would include an overhead source, sconces on the walls, and an accent light on a piece of artwork at the end of the hallway to draw your eye toward your destination.

- **Automated Controls:** Smart home devices are easy to find and more affordable than ever, and they can provide incredible convenience. Wouldn't it be nice to turn the lights on *before* you arrive home so you can feel secure and welcomed? Look for a system that lets you preset different lighting combinations so it's easy to set the desired mood with the push of a button.

- **Light the Landscape:** When it's dark outside and light inside, your windows become mirrors, which can be disconcerting. Train an outdoor spotlight on a lovely tree or other feature, and you make the windows transparent again. Being able to see your landscape boosts your sense of earth-grounding, and outdoor LEDs don't use any more electricity than a nightlight.

OPENING YOUR EARS: ADDRESSING YOUR HOME'S SOUNDSCAPE

We're often so focused on what our homes *look* like that we neglect our other senses—but this is a mistake. Stray sounds are often pebbles, and all irritating noises should be muffled in the well-centered home: droning appliances, the rush of air from the heating system, the Niagara-like sound of a toilet flushing upstairs. Even if you have grown accustomed to them, these sounds still disrupt your mind's effort to sort stimuli and become centered.

Think of it this way: The well-centered home is like meditation: it calms the mind. But just as loud sounds would disrupt you during a meditation session, so too do they interrupt the flow of calming energy in the well-centered home.

Common Sound Pebbles to Address

- **Sound-Insulate Interior Walls:** You can suppress sounds transmitted through the walls by adding insulation to the cavities between the studs. You can also replace the drywall with high-density drywall, or add a layer of mass-loaded vinyl behind new drywall. This is labor-intensive and best done as part of new construction. If you are unable or unwilling to rebuild the walls, tapestries or insulated curtains can improve paper-thin walls in a pinch.

- **Replace Hollow-Core Doors:** Hollow doors allow a great deal of sound transmission between rooms, but you can dampen that by adding solid doors. This is more affordable than redoing the walls, and they also look and feel much better.

- **Muffle Noisy Pipes:** PVC waste pipes are inexpensive for builders, but they can cause a rushing waterfall sound when the toilet flushes. For new construction, pay a bit extra to have the plumber install cast iron pipes on the vertical segments instead. If you have an existing condition, it might be worth opening the wall and wrapping the pipe with strips of mass-loaded vinyl. Whatever you do, do not use spray foam—it will actually amplify the sound.

- **Address Buzzing Electronics:** Many devices emit a high-pitched hum. If you're older, you may not be able to hear it, but if you do, think about where you store and charge your electronics, especially at night. LED lights can also cause a buzzing sound when used on old-fashioned dimmer switches, so be sure to purchase dimmable LEDs and get correctly sized dimmers to avoid this annoyance.

$ Quick Tip

Lively acoustics are welcome in a concert hall, but not in the bedroom and other meditative spaces. Add carpeting, curtains, and other plush textiles to help dampen the liveliness of hard surfaces and create a more peaceful environment.

Sound Pearls to Enhance Your Enjoyment

- **Add a Water Feature:** An indoor water feature doesn't need to be large to be effective. The brain interprets the sound of water as non-threatening, which helps you slip into a state of relaxation.[11] As your brain moves toward a theta state, you are also more creative and receptive to the free flow of

---

[11] Hadhazy, Adam. "Why Does the Sound of Water Help You Sleep?" *Live Science.* Jan. 18, 2016. Accessed Mar. 26, 2020. https://www.livescience.com/53403-why-sound-of-water-helps-you-sleep.html

ideas.[12] Also, gentle water sounds can mask other irritating sounds you can't control by other means.

- **Connect to Nature's Sounds:** Remember that a good deal of earth-grounding happens through your ears, so open the windows to let in birdsong, the sound of leaves rustling in the breeze, or nighttime crickets. I've even had some clients ask for a metal roof on a portion of their house, just so they can enjoy the sound of the rain.

- **Install a Whole-House Sound System:** It's easier than ever to install a wireless sound system that lets you enjoy music in any room. In this way you can listen to nature sounds, soothing music, or just white noise to mask any unpleasant sounds you have identified as pebbles.

FINE-TUNING THERMOCEPTION: HEATING AND COOLING TIPS FOR TOTAL COMFORT

Though sight and sound are by far the most active senses when it comes to taking in stimuli in your home, I would be remiss not to discuss the importance of thermoception—your nervous system's ability to sense hot

---

[12] Hermann, Ned. "What Is the Function of the Various Brainwaves?" *Scientific American*. Dec. 22, 1997. Accessed Mar. 26, 2020. https://www.scientificamerican.com/article/what-is-the-function-of-t-1997-12-22/

and cold via specialized nerves in the skin.[13] This is a crucial sense for survival as well as for your comfort at home.

As we've discussed, a large part of feeling centered in your home is the removal of distractions and discomforts. Thanks to our always-active thermoreceptors, few things are as disruptive to our comfort as a room that is too hot or too cold. For this reason, it's critical to address the heating, ventilating, and air conditioning (HVAC) system in your home to mitigate any problems.

HVAC typically functions as an integrated system, at least in newer homes. You may not look at your furnace or air conditioner very often, but you can feel whether they're functioning as a pebble or a pearl on a daily basis. An improperly functioning or poorly designed HVAC system can be a major pebble that keeps you from enjoying a well-centered home. The temperature, cleanliness, and general comfort of the air in your home should be excellent. Your physical and mental well-being depend on it.

With a good HVAC system, you should not be overly aware of the room's temperature. It should simply feel right. If you notice hot or cold spots, it's likely due to improperly sized ductwork or improperly adjusted dampers that keep air from being balanced across your home. Sometimes a simple adjustment by a qualified HVAC contractor can

---

[13] Zhang, Xuming. "Molecular Sensors and Modulators of Thermoception." *Channels.* Apr. 14, 2015. Accessed Mar. 26, 2020. https://www.ncbi.nlm.nih.gov/pmc/articles/PMC4594430/

rebalance the system and improve things. In more severe cases, alterations to the ductwork may be needed to allow the proper amount of air to get to every room.

Additionally, many houses have plenty of diffusers that blow air into the room, but not enough "return air" grills that let air return to the HVAC equipment. This is especially common in bedrooms, where a lack of air flow is a problem whenever the door is closed for privacy. If old, stale air cannot *leave* the room, newly conditioned air cannot *enter* the room. If the open door is the only way air can leave the room, the blockage created when the door is closed will cause you to feel too cold in the winter and too hot in the summer.

The high-cost cure for this problem is to install a return air grill and duct that connects directly to the home's main ductwork. If that is not feasible, you can install a return air grill in the ceiling above the door, another grill in the ceiling outside the door, and connect the two with a segment of flexible duct to allow air to escape. Put a gentle bend in the flexible duct to reduce the sound that might travel through the duct from hallway to bedroom or vice versa.

It's also a good idea to increase the overall energy efficiency of your home to keep it warmer in the winter and cooler in the summer. Most of the heat loss or gain in a house goes through the ceiling and roof, so adding extra layers of insulation in your attic will limit heat loss or gain for far less than the cost of a new HVAC system. Added insulation will make the temperatures inside your house more uniform and help eliminate cold spots. As home improvements go, additional attic insulation is inexpensive and highly effective. It's also good for the environment, as you'll use less energy to heat and cool your home.

While you're at it, search for and seal up air leaks around your house. Spending a little money on insulation and sealing up your home will cost a lot less than an expensive array of solar panels, and it will pay you back much faster.

Finally, have your HVAC system and ductwork checked for leaks and improper operation. An annual tuneup is a great way to make sure things are in proper working order. Have the technician inspect the entire system and eliminate any rattles, fan sounds, or sounds of rushing air. Those are pebbles you do not need to tolerate. During these visits, ask for recommendations on how often to clean or replace the air filters to keep allergens and mold at bay. A well-centered home must be a healthful as well as comfortable place!

Quick Tip

Nightingale homebody types crave comfort, so proper heating and cooling is especially critical. To enhance control, keep extra blankets available in winter and perhaps a few table fans in summer so individuals can easily adjust according to their personal thermostats.

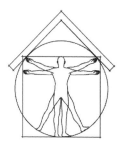

Chapter 11

COLOR MY WORLD:
WHAT HUES AND SHADES
DO FOR OUR HOME—
AND OUR SOULS

P ablo Picasso said, "Colors, like features, follow the changes of the emotions,"[14] something that's well-known among artists, fashion designers, interior designers, and especially advertising consultants. Certain colors trigger predictable emotional responses and have been linked to changes in blood pressure,[15]

---

[14] *Pablo Picasso: Paintings, Quotes and Biography.* Accessed 7 Apr. 2020 at https://www.pablopicasso.org/quotes.jsp

[15] Kutchma, Theresa M. "The Effects of Room Color on Stress Perception: Red Versus Green Environments." *Journal of Undergraduate Research at Minnesota State University, Mankato.* 2003. Accessed 7 Apr. 2020 at https://cornerstone.lib.mnsu.edu/cgi/viewcontent. cgi?article=1172&context=jur

appetite,[16] and even eye strain.[17] Color is powerful; it plays a major role in how centered you feel in your home.

A BRIEF HISTORY OF COLOR IN SCIENCE AND CULTURE

For millennia, colors have been associated with different meanings and powers. In ancient Egypt, artists used a palette of six colors—not only to add realism to their artwork, but to symbolize various beliefs. For example, green was associated with life and growth, thanks to its association with living things in nature.[18] In traditional Chinese medicine, colors are associated with primary organs of the body and are believed to help in healing these areas and creating a more balanced life.[19] In Western cultures, purple is associated with royalty, because the color was originally so hard to produce that only the wealthiest people could

---

[16] "How Color Affects Your Appetite." *Auguste Escoffier School of Culinary Arts*. 25 Jul. 2013. Accessed 7 Apr. 2020 at https://www. escoffieronline.com/how-color-affects-your-appetite

[17] Heid, Markham. "You Asked: What's the Best Way to Stare at Screens All Day?" *Time*. 24 May 2017. Accessed 7 Apr. 2020 at https:// time.com/4789208/screens-computer-eye-strain/

[18] Mark, Joshua J. "Color in Ancient Egypt." *Ancient History Encyclopedia*. 8 Jan. 2017. Accessed 13 Apr. 2020 at https://www. ancient.eu/article/999/color-in-ancient-egypt/

[19] "What Color Are You?" *Traditional Chinese Medicine World Foundation*. Accessed 13 Apr. 2020 at https://www.tcmworld.org/ what-color-are-you-2/

afford purple robes. Its scarcity made it valuable, and to this day we often think of deep purple as a regal color.

In addition to color's influence over culture, the study of color is a science in its own right. The first systematic look into how colors work was conducted by Sir Isaac Newton. Though he is better known for his exploration of gravity and the physical laws of inertia, Newton was the first to determine that all the colors of the spectrum are present in sunlight and can be refracted with a prism. In 1665, he designed a rudimentary color wheel,[20] which became the basis for the color wheels artists use today to guide their mixing of colors while painting.

Today, psychologists in particular are fascinated by the power of color to influence our moods. Much ancient wisdom has touched upon the unique properties of colors to heal and soothe, but the field of chromatherapy subjects these claims to scientific study. The results have been fascinating.

In one noteworthy example, scientists quantified what many people have already suspected about the color red: that it is associated with high energy, and even aggression and dominance. These researchers found that red uniforms enhance athletes' performance over opponents in blue, a color associated with calm. The same holds true for sports

---

[20] Taylor, Ashley P. "Newton's Color Theory, ca. 1665." *The Scientist.* 28 Feb. 2017. Accessed 13 Apr. 2020 at https://www.the-scientist.com/foundations/newtons-color-theory-ca-1665-31931

in which a judge's opinion matters, further showing that our perception of these colors is universal in nature.[21]

Though the full impact of color on the human psyche has not been tracked by modern science, we instinctively respond to it. All human beings perceive color directly via the specialized nerve endings in the retina, which stimulate nerve activity and then the brain in particular ways. When we understand how color influences us, we can begin to harness it to make our homes places of true relaxation and joy.

Who Is Roy G. Biv?

I was first introduced to Mr. Biv in seventh-grade science class. He is not a real person, but rather a mnemonic device for Sir Isaac Newton's seven primary colors of the spectrum: **R**ed, **o**range, **y**ellow, **G**reen, **B**lue, **i**ndigo, and **v**iolet. Roy G. Biv is the embodiment of Newton's discovery: Remember his name and you will remember the colors in their order in the rainbow.

---

[21] Jones, Jonathan. "Super Bowl 2020 Uniforms: Chiefs' Decision Could Play Key Role in Unprecedented Red vs. Red Game." *CBS Sports*. 2 Feb. 2020. Accessed 13 Apr. 2020 at https://www.cbssports.com/nfl/news/super-bowl-2020-uniforms-chiefs-decision-could-play-key-role-in-unprecedented-red-vs-red-game/

The Psychology of Color

As Goethe pointed out in his influential 1810 book *Theory of Colors*, we all react differently to color,[22] and science can take us only so far into our own subjectivity. But there are clear patterns of feeling that emerge with each color, and understanding the basics about how color influences your mood will help you center your home.

Red

Red is the color of high energy. It's a show-off; it demands attention. It has been shown to raise blood pressure and is associated with danger because of its use in warning signs and emergency vehicles—a cultural connection that cannot be undone. But when used judiciously, red can stimulate human interaction and conversation. Though not a good choice for bedrooms and meditation spaces, red can work in public areas where you plan to entertain. In the evening, when illuminated by the warm shades of artificial light, reds become more subdued and add a feeling of richness and elegance that is especially nice in a dining room or den.

Orange

Like red, orange is a stimulating color that impels you to action, though without the in-your-face intensity and

---

[22] Goethe, Johann Wolfgang von. *Theory of Colors*. Translated by Charles Locke Eastlake. Cambridge: MIT Press, 1970. https://mitpress.mit.edu/books/theory-colours

danger that red can provoke. For this reason, orange may be easier to work with in the home, particularly if you choose hues that reflect autumnal tones found in nature. In ancient cultures, orange was thought to heal the lungs and increase energy levels. For modern homes, the energetic nature of orange is useful in exercise rooms and playrooms.

Yellow

Yellow is the color of sunshine and happiness. It's a good choice for rooms you occupy in the morning, such as the bathroom, the breakfast room, hallways, and foyers. Though it can be cheery, yellow should be used with care, as intense hues can be irritating. Too much yellow can induce feelings of frustration and anger, and in my experience, babies seem to cry more in yellow rooms. Effective use of yellow in the home requires careful balance to avoid tipping from pretty to prickly.

Green

A supremely restful color, green is considered to be easiest on the eye. Because it's found everywhere in nature, it's the ideal color to enhance earth-grounding in the well-centered home. Green creates a sense of relaxation, peace, and warmth. Traditionally, green was the go-to color for hospitals, due to its calming effect. Though "hospital green" is now a cliché, there are so many shades and tones of green that it's easy to find one that presents a fresh face in any room of the home. In addition to encouraging relaxation, green is also believed by some to help with fertility, making it a good choice for the bedroom.

Blue

Blue is the calming Yin to Red's energetic Yang. The soothing color of ocean and sky has been demonstrated to reduce blood pressure and slow the heart rate,[23] making it a beneficial color for bedrooms and bathrooms. Blue can be temperamental, though, with pale tints making rooms without much natural light feel cold and off-putting. Richer tones, particularly blues that tend slightly toward teal or periwinkle, are good for family rooms and open kitchens. Dark blue shades are fine for accents, but they should not be used as the main color in a room because they can provoke sadness.

Purple

In its lighter shades of lilac and lavender, purple is another restful color. Many years of cultural associations also mean that most people regard pale purple as distinctly feminine, so it may not be the best choice for a couple's bedroom. But it can be used with a light touch to enhance

---

[23] Al-Ayash, Aseel, et al. "The Influence of Color on Student Emotion, Heart Rate and Performance in Learning Environments." *Color Research and Application*. Feb. 2015. Accessed 7 Apr. 2020 at https://www.researchgate.net/publication/272890833_The_influence _of_color_on_student_emotion_heart_rate_and_performance_in_ learning_environments

the relaxing qualities of a bathroom if a more spa-like feel is desired. Darker shades of purple are rich and dramatic and still create an impression of regal luxury.

Neutral Tones

These are mild versions of every color, muted and subdued with plenty of gray or tan mixed in. These are also the underlying tones of the hundreds of versions of "white" you'll find at the paint store. When choosing neutrals, be mindful of those underlying colors and the qualities they evoke. You might not perceive the color as much, but its power to affect your mood will still be there, so consider carefully whether you'd prefer a warm neutral that has a few drops of red or yellow in the mix, or a cooler neutral with a bit of blue in the mix. If you're not sure what you're seeing, you can ask the paint manager to look up the exact formula to show you how much of any given color is used to make that particular paint.

A PLEASING COLOR PALETTE FOR EVERY HOMEBODY TYPE

Once you understand how colors can make you feel, you're ready to put that knowledge to use to select colors for your home. Still, there are literally thousands of shades and tints of any given color. If you don't believe me, think of the last time you tried to describe a shade of turquoise to someone. I'll bet you said something like "greener than the sky, but bluer than sea glass, and not as intense as the ocean," or something to that effect. Each of the basic colors listed above has so many variations that it can be hard to know where to start. Exactly which shade of yellow will make you happy? Which blue will help you relax and drift off to sleep?

To help you begin selecting colors to balance the energy in your home, I asked my favorite interior designer and artist, Agnes Preston Brame, www.paintingsbyapb.com, to put together a few colors that would be appropriate to each homebody type. Agnes has a real gift for color. She has spent years looking for perfect fabric colors as a consultant for textile manufacturers, and she has a deep understanding of how colors interact with each other to form a pleasing, balanced whole.

Once I explained each homebody's basic personality to Agnes, she created collections of colors that work well together and would make them feel perfectly relaxed at home. You can use these color collections throughout your home with confidence, knowing they will blend beautifully and help center your home in ways that resonate with your personality.

The color palettes listed below are based on Benjamin Moore color choices. Other paint companies will have similar offerings, or they can computer-match any color you provide as a reference. Each palette has five wall colors and a trim color that will work with all the colors in the collection.

The Astaire Palette: Bold Hues for the Entertainer

For the walls:

- Deep Mulberry (BM 2069-10)

- Rosy Apple (BM 2006-30)

- Concord Ivory (BM HC-12)

- Yukon Sky (BM 1439)

- Shaker Beige (BM HC-45)

For the trim:

- Mountain Peak White (BM 2148-70)

The Galileo Palette: Neutral Tones for the Scientist

For the walls:

- Iron Mountain (BM 2134-30)

- Desert Twilight (BM 2137-40)

- Sea Haze (BM 2137-50)

- Van Courtland Blue (BM HC-145)

- Coastal Fog (BM AC-1)

For the trim:

- Glacier White (BM AC-40)

The Nightingale Palette: Calm Colors for the Nurturer

For the walls:

- Mill Springs Blue (BM HC-137)

- Spring Valley (BM 438)

- Beacon Hill Damask (BM HC-2)

- Persian Melon (BM 117)

- White Rain (BM 708)

For the trim:

- Meadow Mist (BM 936)

The Plato Palette: Natural Shades for the Philosopher

For the walls:

- Clinton Brown (BM HC-67)

- Maryville Brown (BM HC-75)

- Copper Mountain (BM AC-12)

- Springfield Tan (BM AC-5)

- Mistletoe (BM 474)

For the trim:

- Gentle Cream (BM OC-96)

As you consider these palettes, remember that no one is 100 percent a particular homebody type. These palettes are meant to provide inspiration, not to limit you in any way.

Practical Color Advice From an Interior Designer

While I was working with my friend Agnes on the color palettes for the homebody types, she shared several great tips for making the most of these color schemes in your home. Agnes' advice was too good not to pass along, so I've compiled her pearls of wisdom here.

1. Don't forget that the colors in each palette are applicable for all items in the room: upholstery, window treatments, rugs, accessories, etc. Those items do not need to precisely match the suggested colors. Just use these colors as a guide for hues of those other items, and you'll easily put together a cohesive look in your room.

2. If you prefer a white room and plan to use your homebody color palette for furniture and other accessories, choose the suggested trim color in a flat finish for the walls and semi-gloss for the trim. The different sheens will make the painted surfaces appear to be slightly different colors, but they will be impeccably compatible.

continued on the next page...

Practical Color Advice From an Interior Designer
...continued

3. When assembling a room based on a color palette, start with the floor. Rugs, carpets, and other floor finishes have the strongest impact on the room. The wall paint comes next, and finally the accessories should follow suit. In this way, you will start with the "base" that covers your whole room and work your way up and out to the details.

4. When in doubt, black is always a good accent color. It will be compatible with any of the color suggestions in your palette, and nearly any item you add to your home, from electronics to light fixtures, will be available in basic black.

5. Don't forget to add an element of surprise to the room—not every item has to match a tone in your suggested color palette. Use your own judgment to add a new color to the mix, and let yourself have some fun with this. Accessories are ideal for experimentation because they are easily moved elsewhere if you change your mind.

TIPS FOR USING COLOR EFFECTIVELY IN THE WELL-CENTERED HOME

Once you have selected colors that fit your personality and create your desired energy in each room of your home, your work isn't quite complete. There are still some fine points to consider to make sure your colors create a soothing, harmonious palette. Here are some of the most important lessons I've learned about working with color over the years.

Ensure Smooth Transitions

We've already discussed the importance of smooth progressions from indoor-to-outdoor and public-to-private spaces, and the same holds true for the use of colors. You want to avoid sudden, jarring contrasts between rooms or within a single room. For example, you wouldn't want to go step from a pale blue room into a bright red hallway.

The best way to ensure effective color transitions is to make sure that the colors of adjacent rooms work together in a harmonious palette. This is easily done if you choose one of the homebody palettes listed above, or you can test your own palettes with paint chips. To do this, stand in one room and note all the other rooms you can see from that vantage point. Gather paint chips for all the rooms you can see and place them together in your hand to make sure they blend nicely. You can repeat this for every room in the house to check your color transitions and help you choose hues that work well together.

Choose the Sheen Wisely

Color isn't the only consideration when choosing paint. The sheen, or reflectivity of the finish, is almost as important. Flat or matte paints are the least reflective, while eggshell and satin reflect more light. Semigloss and gloss finishes are the most reflective. The shinier the finish, the more energetic your room will seem—and the more the light will bounce off the surfaces to create different tones of your paint color.

Interior designers are in love with eggshell finishes for the drama they provide, but glossier paints have a big drawback: They are impossible to touch up without showing where the old paint ends and the new paint begins, and they show every imperfection in the walls. It's true that glossier paints are easier to clean, but they make "scrubbable" flat paints now, too. A matte finish will save you a lot of time and money on spackling and sanding walls to perfection, and it will allow you to make small touch-ups and repairs on your own without being forced to recoat the entire wall.

Check the Undertones in "White" Paints

Many people assume that white is the easiest, most foolproof color, but white isn't purely white. Paint stores have hundreds of shades of white, and hints of subtle, underlying hues are present in every one of them. These undertones show up once you paint an entire room with a so-called "white." Have you ever had the experience of painting a room white only to find it turned pink or blue along the way? Those tones that were imperceptible on the paint chip now show through once light can reflect from one wall to the next, effectively amplifying the tonal effect.

To select the ideal shade of white for your room, look at the color chart for that white. What are the deeper versions of that color further down on the card? Pay attention to these pigments, because they are the secret color buried in the white. Make sure these deeper tones work with your overall color palette, and you'll be pleased with the results—even when your room looks less white in certain lights than you expected.

Seek a Professional Opinion

After years of working with clients on finishing their homes, I have come to the conclusion that true color aptitude is a rare thing, and it can take years to develop an artist's eye for color in all its subtlety. If you're having any doubts at all about your color selections, consult with a talented interior designer. A great designer has used many, many paint colors in the past and knows what they look like in real rooms. Designers will have a go-to list of "dependable" colors that always work, and an hour or two of professional color review will be money very well spent.

Always Paint Samples on the Walls

One small sample of a color on a card with a white border will look very different in your hand than it does on the wall. There are several reasons for this. First, the border color affects the way your brain interprets the color: a square of yellow on a green background looks different than the same shade of yellow on a white background, so context matters. Second, the undertones that we spoke of in white paints also exist in other colors, and they will intensify when that small paint chip is scaled up to four walls' worth of color. Painting a *large* sample will help you get a more realistic sense of the color's intensity.

It's also important to live with that color sample for several days. This will allow you to experience the hue at different times of day to see how changing patterns of daylight affect it. A buttery yellow may be pleasant in soft morning light, but garish in the afternoon. Likewise, colors will look different as the seasons change: The angle of the sun and seasonal changes in greenery outside your windows will affect how your colors reflect the light. Be sure you see your wall sample at all times of day and in several different types of weather before committing.

Be Judicious With Accent Colors

Just as a jumble of too many items can cause visual chaos, so too can a jumble of different colors. If you put every color in every room, your emotional energy will be broken up and scattered about as your mind tries to keep up with so many disparate elements at once. This will work against your goal of creating a calm, comfortable place.

To avoid de-centering yourself with color, it's very helpful to start with a basic palette. Not every item needs to match exactly, and you can certainly have a few accessories that stray from the plan. But in general, the fewer colors you have in your room, the more peaceful it will feel—even if those colors are rich and bold.

Work Carefully With Gray

Gray is a wonderful neutral that helps mute strong colors. It's the happy medium that helps unite and blend accent colors in your palette, so it definitely has a place in every home. We tend to let gray slide into the background as a "non-color," but nothing could be further from the truth. Just like all those different versions of white, gray has undertones that you need to be aware of.

There are two categories of gray: warm grays, which have a hint of tan or brown in them, and cool grays, which have a hint of blue. They are the oil and water of the world of color. They must never be mixed! You can have a gray room that is very warm and inviting if you use warm shades of French gray, which is a doeskin type of color. But you cannot combine French gray with a color like cadet blue or another cool, steely shade of gray. They'll always be at war with each other, and the clash will unsettle your well-centered home.

Don't Be Afraid of Bold Color

Strong colors can provide more power and energy in a room. There's a reason the design magazines rarely feature interiors that are meek and washed out. If you're feeling nervous, consider painting only one wall in the rich accent color and use the "white" version of the color on the other walls. Choosing that version of white guarantees your other walls will play nicely with the accent wall.

Finally, do remember that it's only paint. This is the easiest thing to change in your home, so don't be afraid to experiment—you might surprise yourself with the beneficial results. If you make a mistake and a paint choice becomes a pebble, the only thing it will cost you is another can of paint and a few hours to try again to create the pearl you wanted.

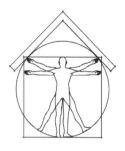

Chapter 12

BRINGING JOY TO MIND: USING OBJECTS, ART, AND OTHER DESIGN ELEMENTS TO CREATE HAPPINESS

Your degree of joyfulness in life is directly related to how you respond to the world around you. Any aspect of your home that triggers a joyful response is a pearl, and you want to cultivate as many pearls as you can.

We were all born into the world with an innate capacity for joy. Very young children instinctively react to things with pure happiness—just think of the hearty belly laugh a toddler lets fly while playing, and you know what I mean. But as life progresses, our experiences tend to dampen that joy and cause us to become cynical and suspicious. There is a tendency to recall negative events more readily than positive ones.

Joy relies on the absence of negativity, so removing negatives and amplifying positives are the keys to making your home a joyful, well-centered place. It's all about eliminating pebbles and adding pearls.

Our behavior also influences our joy. It's hard to feel happy when frowning, and it's hard to be unhappy when smiling. Try it sometime! Those simple facial expressions reflect our emotions, but they also stimulate them. By the same token, if your home is bland and full of pebbles, it is unlikely to bring joy, no matter how great your mood was when you walked in the door. On the other hand, if your home flows easily, aligns with the world around it, and contains objects that remind you of happy times, it's hard to remain joyless even on the worst days.

THE FINE ART OF PERSONALIZING YOUR HOME

Most of the pearls that trigger a joyful response are personal. After all, you have individual relationships and life experiences that are unique to *you*. You also have an innate temperament, personality, and tastes to consider. While there are some universal triggers for happiness—decluttering, natural light, earth-grounding—your unique triggers are the strongest.

But there's a fine line between adding pearls and overwhelming your space with visual clutter. Decorative objects should always be added in a measured way. A luscious dessert brings instant gratification, but too many desserts will have ill effects on your digestion and your waistline.

Likewise, too much of a good thing—whether souvenirs from abroad or treasured family photos—will spoil your well-centered home. You don't want objects competing for your attention, so keep in mind the lessons on visual rhythms from Chapter 9. You want to remain focused on the energy you create with your decorative items to avoid busyness and overstimulation.

The best decor, then, adds pearls to remind you of happy times throughout your life while maintaining the careful balance of color, pattern, and other elements you've achieved in your well-centered home.

The Power of Contrast and Context

As part of creating schema for understanding the world, we judge and categorize everything around us by comparing it to things we have already experienced. How does one thing compare and contrast with another? How does something blend in or stand out in its context? Our experiences

continued on the next page...

The Power of Contrast and Context

...continued

provide the yardstick by which we measure the world around us.

To understand how contrast and context work, consider a five-year-old. He looks tall and sturdy when standing next to his baby sister, but that same five-year-old looks tiny standing next to his mother. How we perceive the child depends a lot on where he is and who he's with—in other words, the context of the scene.

You can use the principles of contrast and context to help create effective focal points and increase the impact of certain spaces in your home. For example, a narrow hallway painted in a dark color will make the rooms it leads to feel larger and brighter upon entry. Objects with strong colors stand out more in rooms with a neutral color as a background, but lose their oomph when surrounded by other brightly colored objects.

To make the most of the power of contrast, it helps to think of yourself as the director of a play. In each room, determine what object is to be the lead actor, and help it shine in its role by selecting other objects to serve as supporting actors and extras. Extras should

continued on the next page...

...continued

form a pleasing background without competing
for the eye's focus, while supporting players
can play off of the star of the show, visually
speaking.

THE HAPPINESS QUOTIENT: HOW TO ASSESS THE OBJECTS IN YOUR HOME

To get that balance right, you will need to actively
choose the decor items you wish to display. I've written
a good deal in this book about the need to look at your
home with a fresh perspective, but nowhere is that more
important than in selecting the objects you rely on to bring
a daily dose of delight.

To do this, try "auditioning" a few items at a time by
placing them in a very prominent location for a few days.
Put a painting, photographs, or a collection of one to three
related items on display where you will see them several
times a day. Good locations for your audition space are on
top of the mantel, in your foyer, or at the end of a hallway
you traverse often—depending, of course, on whether the
items require wall space or a shelf.

After the third or fourth day of your test run, consider
how you feel about those decorative objects. Do they make
you smile when you see them? Do they make you think of
someone you care about? Do they remind you of a happy

time or an interesting trip you took? While photographs of children or grandchildren never lose their power to bring joy, other objects might grow less interesting with more frequent exposure. Keep your eyes—and your heart—open, and have an honest conversation with yourself about how each item makes you feel.

Use the results of this audition to determine how prominently the items might be displayed. The objects that unfailingly bring happiness to your life should be housed in places of honor, while items with less impact can be placed in less obvious locations or packed away entirely.

This exercise should help you build confidence in your ability to evaluate your possessions and discern which ones resonate best in your well-centered home. While putting your belongings in a different context for a few days helps you see them with new eyes, you'll probably begin to see a pattern in the types of decorative items you respond to most strongly. As your preferences take clearer shape, you can move on from the auditioning phase and simply scan your room to note the items that will work best in your home decor.

Quick Tip

Of all the homebody types, Galileos have the lowest tolerance for visual clutter. These homebody types should conduct object auditions one item at a time. Galileos are likely to be happy with a few meaningful focal points instead of trying to arrange a full gallery wall or a shelf full of objects.

DECOR THAT DELIGHTS FOR EVERY HOMEBODY TYPE

Though everyone will have a unique combination of items that make them happy, each homebody type has a few go-to items that are sure to work with the energy they've cultivated in their homes. If you're not certain where to begin—or if you're looking for a few additional items to round out your personal collection and put the finishing touch on a space—try these tried-and-true tips.

For Everyone

Some things just make everyone happier. Universal triggers for joy include simplifying the world around you and maintaining calm instead of chaos. For a refresher on removing the major pebbles of visual clutter, refer to Chapter 7.

For most people, redecorating and rearranging also bring joy, because they force you to engage with your decor with a fresh perspective. The simple act of changing your home environment makes you more attuned to it. Your perception will be intensified, which leads to a stronger connection to the items you've chosen to bring a smile to your face and your heart.

Artwork, photographs, and objects that connect you to other people are always excellent choices for creating decor that makes you happy. Items that make you nostalgic for the past—whether from your personal history or a bygone era—trigger powerful memories and emotions for everyone.

One final item that never fails in home decor: fresh flowers. They're a wonderful way to enhance peopling and earth-grounding while adding a burst of seasonal color to any room. It's nearly impossible to be unhappy with fresh flowers on the table.

For Astaire Homebody Types

Astaire types enjoy having an audience. While it's not possible to be constantly entertaining others, the next best thing is to surround yourself with photographs that commemorate happy events from the past. Consider photos from parties and performances, or souvenirs from group gatherings or travels. Displaying awards or other mementos of recognition will also provide Astaire types the social energy they thrive on.

For Galileo Homebody Types

Because Galileo types thrive on mental stimulation, mementos from schools and universities will remind them of their happiest times, so hang diplomas in a place of honor. Galileo types tend to be passionately devoted to career or hobbies, so reminders of these deep interests will also create joyful decor throughout the home.

For Nightingale Homebody Types

Nurturing Nightingale types thrive when surrounded by reminders of family and friends. In addition to photographs, consider choosing artwork or crafts made by people you know. Religious imagery or artwork that displays meaningful quotations may also work well for Nightingale types, as these messages warm the heart and offer inspiration not just to you, but to anyone who enters your home.

For Plato Homebody Types

Philosophical Plato types enjoy decor with a sense of history attached. Antiques, ancient relics, and objects related to family heritage will spark contemplation, their preferred mental state. Abstract art and sculpture are also good choices for Plato types, who prefer to meditate on the world's possibilities rather than just its realities.

TIPS FOR MAINTAINING BALANCE IN YOUR PERSONAL DECOR

If the idea of removing some personal items from your decor has you sick at heart, don't worry. No one is suggesting that you permanently eliminate something you love! If you have more things than you have places, rotate them throughout the year. This gives you opportunities to see items in a fresh way, and you'll add positive energy to your life through the simple act of rearranging.

For most people, it makes sense to change decor seasonally. You may already change your decor on a small scale: you may decorate for the holidays or swap out table linens for different themes throughout the year. But you can also seasonally rotate the beloved items on your shelves or mantel to achieve a new look. Try setting a reminder on your phone to swap out decor at the start of each season to give yourself a little pick-me-up and allow new items to shine in a place of honor. Synchronizing your activities with seasonal changes goes a long way toward linking your inner energies to the cycles of the earth and sun as well.

Though imagery of family and friends is universally appealing, the sheer number of photos we collect can become overwhelming. Electronic picture frames are a great solution; they allow you to display numerous important photos sequentially in the same spot.

If you prefer printed and framed photographs, it's important to group them together carefully to prevent visual chaos. Display them on one wall as a composed arrangement that entices the eye to move from one to another. Hallway walls are good places for these galleries. For best results, place the center of the grouping 57 to 60 inches above the floor, the optimum height for artwork. Some individual pictures can be higher or lower, but the center of the arrangement is the key locating point. Test out the arrangement by laying out the pictures on the floor before banging nails into the wall. Let your eye be your guide, but take time to think it through so the overall composition is balanced and pleasing.

When placing objects, keep in mind that smaller items may not be dominant enough to stand alone in a space. If that's the case, you'll need to create arrangements for a display with a pleasing scale. Balanced groups of three items work well. If the objects are unequal in size, place the tallest in the middle with the others on either side.

Don't be afraid to have uneven spaces between items, especially if the other two objects are not identical in size—lining things up like toy soldiers never looks right. Experiment with moving one closer or farther away until they "read" as a group and your eye moves smoothly from one to the next. For more advice about creating visual rhythms with your objects and collections, refer back to Chapter 9.

If you're looking for the perfect place to display your favorite things, look around your home to find its focal points—the places where your eye naturally comes to rest as you scan the room. Good spots include the following:

- straight ahead at the end of a hallway

- directly opposite from the doorway entering a room

- directly across from your seating area

- on your vanity next to the sink where you will notice it morning and night

- near your home's main entryway

By choosing these pieces of prime visual real estate, you'll give yourself every chance to catch a glimpse of these important generators of joy and happiness each and every day.

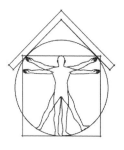

Chapter 13

LIVING IN AND LOVING YOUR WELL-CENTERED HOME

Throughout the course of this book, you've learned to think like an architect as you explore your home's impact on your well-being. A well-centered home, much like meditation, provides a sense of calm. By understanding how the design and furnishing of your home influence your senses, you can carefully assess it, and then choose pebbles to remove and pearls to add. By opening your eyes and training your mind to receive the energy all around you, you'll develop an entirely new relationship with your home.

As you begin this valuable work, there are three important points to remember:

1. **Your home is a channel for energy.** This is the energy within you and the energy of the universe all around you. It is powerful!

2. **Your home can either disturb or reinforce this energy.** You can direct this energy based on how your home is oriented on the earth, how the spaces are arranged, and how the objects and finishes you select interact with each other.

3. **Even small changes make a big impact.** One tiny adjustment can yield big results as you harness your home's energy and increase your own mindfulness in your space.

Before You Embark on Your Journey, Know Your Destination

If there is a "Golden Rule of Home Centering," it is this:

Do the things YOU like. Don't be overly influenced by others.

You are the best yardstick for measuring how well your home is centered, so always work to please yourself. If it works for you, then it works.

But a word of caution: Though you are the final arbiter of your own good taste, you still need a plan. If you go about adding pearls or choosing paint colors without any thought to the overall effect you wish to achieve, you most likely won't be pleased with the results.

I like to say that if you don't know where you're going, you won't know when you get there. A journey is not a journey without a destination. Without a goal, you're just walking around aimlessly. This is just as true in your home as it is on a family vacation with a car full of kids impatiently asking, "Are we there yet?"

It's critical that you define and understand what you're trying to achieve in your home. Otherwise, your efforts will amount to nothing more than rearranging the furniture. To guide your journey, you need an action plan to serve as your road map. Your vision of a well-centered home is the destination.

Putting It All Together: Your Action Plan

So how, exactly, should you approach the rewarding work of centering your home? Your road map consists of four basic steps that you can apply to your entire home, to a particular room, or to your outdoor space.

Step One

Make an objective assessment of your home in its present condition. Walk through your home and look around to get in touch with your emotions. How does each room make you feel? Try to look at all aspects of the space and evaluate whether the components of each room contribute positively or negatively to your emotions. Strive to understand what aspects are preventing it from being well-centered so you can begin to plan your work.

Your Home Assessment Checklist

Throughout this book we've discussed many exercises to help you evaluate your space. Use this checklist as you work to achieve a greater understanding of the energy in each room.

- **Anchoring:** Use a compass and map application to better understand your home's place in the universe. (Chapter 3)

- **View Finding:** Open all window coverings and assess the views to begin earth-grounding. (Chapter 3)

- **Tuning in to the Senses:** Sit in your room and become attuned to how all five senses are affected by the space. (Chapter 4 and Chapter 10)

- **Taking Photographs:** Take photos of each room, then look over them as if they were part of a real estate listing, to

continued on the next page...

Your Home Assessment Checklist

...continued

gain a clearer perspective on pebbles that detract from your space. (Chapter 4)

- **Proofreading:** Take a moment to feel the energy of each object in every room. Was it made by machine or by hand? Does it remind you of joyous times? (Chapter 5)

- **Progressing:** Walk through your home to determine whether you have appropriate spacing between public and private areas. (Chapter 6)

- **Scanning:** Sit in the center of the room and allow your eye to wander. Are there clear focal points upon which your eye can rest? (Chapter 7)

- **Sketching:** Print out the photos you took of each room and turn them upside down. Then draw the shapes you see to determine which forms speak to you. (Chapter 8)

- **Touching:** Review the texture and sensation of materials in your room to get a better sense of the energy they impart and how they interact with each other. (Chapter 8)

continued on the next page...

Your Home Assessment Checklist

...continued

- **Evaluating Patterns:** Allow your eye to wander naturally over any patterns in your home to assess how quickly your eye moves. This reveals the energy of each pattern. (Chapter 9)

- **Color Auditing:** Walk into a room with your eyes looking down so you don't see the walls and furniture. Pretend you have never been in the room before, then look up. Note which colors draw your attention and what emotions they evoke. (Chapter 11)

- **Auditioning:** Place a few objects in a high-traffic location to evaluate how much joy they bring to you each day. Keep the best ones in your decor year-round, or rotate seasonally among several favorites. (Chapter 12)

Step Two

Define your own homebody type so as to better understand your personal preferences and inclinations. If you haven't already done so, take the Homebody Type Quiz in Chapter 2. As you read through your results, remember that no one is entirely one homebody type—we all have secondary tendencies toward another type as well. The quiz is not meant to categorize you, but rather to help you understand more about your personality to harness your home's energy in ways that feel just right.

Step Three

Start the process of adjusting and modifying your home. When you begin work in a new area, start by addressing the conditions or items that cause negative reactions. Remember, you must always remove the pebbles to bring your home's influence on you to a neutral condition. No amount of redecorating will completely cover over a problem that annoys you, so it's crucial to take care of the pebbles in your shoe first. This lays the groundwork for adding beauty and positive energy later.

Step Four

Finally, look for opportunities to add positive aspects to your home. These are the pearls that will transform your space from simply functional to a personal retreat that supports you at every turn. As you work to add pearls, it's most important to focus on your home's anchoring and earth-grounding, as these are the key ways we connect to the earth's energy. Once you have done this, you can continue to add pearls in the form of private retreats, smooth progressions between areas, and delightful forms, shapes, and colors.

ACHIEVING THE WELL-CENTERED HOME

How will you know when you have finally arrived at your ultimate destination—the well-centered home? If you feel yourself becoming more relaxed, if being in your home makes you smile, and if you perceive an overall sense of calm when you are in your home, you have achieved your goal. You won't just like what you see—you'll like how you feel.

Your home should be the place that recharges your emotional batteries. It should provide psychological security and protect you from the onslaughts of everyday life. It should make you happy. It should help you direct your awareness inward to better understand yourself. All of these benefits are possible when you balance the energy around you to create a well-centered home.

Made in the USA
Middletown, DE
17 October 2020